D1457333

MEXICAN WORKERS AND AMERICAN DREAMS

CLASS AND CULTURE

A series edited by

Milton Cantor and Bruce Laurie

MEXICAN WORKERS
AND
AMERICAN DREAMS

Immigration, Repatriation,
and California Farm Labor,
1900–1939

CAMILLE GUERIN-GONZALES

RUTGERS UNIVERSITY PRESS
New Brunswick, New Jersey

Library of Congress Cataloging-in-Publication Data

Guerin-Gonzales, Camille.
  Mexican workers and American dreams : immigration, repatriation,
and California farm labor, 1900–1939 / Camille Guerin-Gonzales.
      p. cm. — (Class and culture)
  Includes bibliographical references and index.
  ISBN 0-8135-2047-9 (cloth) — ISBN 0-8135-2048-7 (pbk.)
  1. Agricultural laborers, Mexican—California—History—20th
century. 2. Mexican American agricultural laborers—California—
History—20th century. 3. California—Emigration and immigration—
History—20th century. 4. Mexico—Emigration and immigration—
History—20th century. 5. Repatriation—Mexico—History—20th
century. I. Title. II. Series.
HD1527.C2G84 1994
331.54′4′0979409041—dc20   93-24223
                                                                CIP

British Cataloging-in-Publication information available

For Susan

CONTENTS

ACKNOWLEDGMENTS

There are many, many people who have made this study possible. Carlos Cortés challenged me always to do just a bit more than I thought I was capable of. His integrity and his own personal commitment to social justice served as a standard against which I could judge my own work. I thank, also, Van Perkins for his careful reading of two of the chapters in the manuscript.

I am deeply grateful to David Brody for the many readings he gave this study in its early form, for allowing me to use his office one summer in Berkeley, for being such an inspiration to me through his writings and our discussions, and for his kindness over the years. I thank David Montgomery for being so generous with his time and his ideas, for his comments on early drafts of the manuscript, and for being so very *simpático*. My friendship with Deena González has been a great source of strength to me. Thank you, Deena, for the intellectual and emotional support you have given me over the years, and for the principled stands you have taken on issues central to the lives of our people, for your courage, and for your sense of honor. Elizabeth Griffin, Alice Wexler, Deena González, Wendy Kozol, Robin Kelley, Vicki Ruiz, Keith Jones, Patricia Limerick, Sharon Salinger, and Harry Lawton read various drafts of the manuscript, and I am very grateful to them for their comments and suggestions for revisions. A number of friends and fellow-travelers, in addition to those I have already mentioned, gave me their friendship and support, and inspired me through their own work. Andrew Feffer, Devra Weber, David Gutiérrez, Carl Strikwerda, Caroline Hinkley, Bette Quinn, Martha Olney, June O'Connor, Kenneth Barkin, Barbara Robinson, Elizabeth Lord, Joan Carlson, Rosalia Solórzano, Gloria Watkins, Refugio Rochin, and Antonia Castañeda have enriched my life and my work in these and many more ways. Ana Castillo took me into her *sanctuaria* so that I could write the introduction. Thank you, Ana, for our talks and for the peacefulness of your home. Judy Baca has been very important to me and I am grateful to her for her kindness and generosity, and, most of all, for the beauty, strength, and power she brings to our people.

My thanks, also, to Connie Young, who made my research and writing much easier. Marlie Wasserman and Marilyn Campbell at Rutgers University Press and Milton Cantor, series editor, have been more patient than anyone could expect, and I thank them for their fortitude with this project and for their insightful comments. I am also very grateful to Julie Tuason for her careful copyediting and indexing and for the work she did to make this a stronger book.

A Fulbright Grant, a dissertation fellowship at the University of California at Santa Barbara, funding from the National Endowment for the Humanities, a postdoctoral fellowship at the University of California at Davis and another at the University of California at Berkeley, and a Ford Foundation Fellowship for Minorities provided the crucial financial support for the research and writing of the manuscript. Institutional support from the Institute of Industrial Relations at the University of California at Berkeley, the History Department at the University of California at Riverside, and the History Department and the American Studies Program at Yale University made it possible for me to work in an intellectually stimulating environment during important phases of the project. Oberlin College provided generous support for research and publication of this book.

The staff at the Bancroft Library, the National Archives and Research Service in Washington, D.C., the Secretaria de Relaciones Exteriores and the Archivo Nacional de México in Mexico City, and the Graduate Research Library at the University of California at Los Angeles were invaluable to this study. I am especially grateful to Richard Ogar and Dan Johnston at the Bancroft Library for their help with the illustrations for this book.

I will never be able to express my gratitude adequately to my daughter, Kerrie Chappell, who gave me her love and encouragement over the years and sustained me in this project. My sons, Ron and Mike Lester, always believed I would finish the book and showed me over and over again that there is more to life than writing history, as have my grandchildren, Casey, Mason, Courtney, and Michael.

This book is dedicated to Susan Johnson. She, more than anyone, made it possible for me to complete this book by opening up a new way of seeing and being for me. I thank her for sharing her ideas with me, for her friendship and strength, for her laughter and smiles, and, most of all, for living her life so passionately.

MEXICAN WORKERS AND
AMERICAN DREAMS

INTRODUCTION

More than a million Mexican immigrant workers traveled north to the United States in the years 1900–1930, settling mainly in the Southwest. Nearly all worked as agricultural wage laborers at one time or another, many on California farms. In the 1930s, this northward movement reversed, as half a million immigrants and Americans of Mexican descent became targets of one of the largest mass-removal operations ever sanctioned by the United States government. Immigration and repatriation both invigorated and disrupted the lives of Mexicans and Mexican Americans, as well as the lives of other ethnic groups in the United States.

Mexican immigrants brought with them ideas, experiences, and cultural practices that other groups, including Mexican Americans, incorporated into their social and economic lives. Immigrants altered residential and employment patterns. Their presence sometimes made it possible for communities to survive and even to thrive, while at other times their competition for housing and jobs had a destabilizing effect on both Mexican and Anglo communities. Mexicans who returned south to Mexico periodically and who maintained contact with family and friends in both the United States and Mexico engaged in a cultural conversation that enriched the lives of people in both countries.

At the same time, return migration devastated the lives of many immigrants and nonimmigrants. Voluntary return, deportation, repatriation, and mass removal destabilized communities on both sides of the border. Mexican immigrants in the United States, as well as Americans who could be mistaken for immigrants, lived in constant fear of expulsion during the 1930s. Entire neighborhoods and communities were destroyed in that decade, when county and state agencies, with the blessing of the federal government, organized the mass removal of Mexican immigrants and Mexican Americans from towns and cities all over the United States. Mexican removal and the publicity that attended the programs affected an entire generation of Mexican immigrants and Mexican Americans, who saw their dreams of making a life for themselves and their children either destroyed or seriously threatened.

Mexican immigrants came to the United States with hopes and dreams shaped by the rhetoric of employment agents in the U.S., Mexican stories and songs glorifying economic opportunities in *el norte*, and popular ideas prevalent in Mexico since the American Revolution about the U.S. as a model of liberal idealism.[1] Although Mexican immigrants encountered and believed in a variety of ideas about America, the language of the American Dream in particular shaped their expectations and behavior. The American Dream promised economic opportunity and security—which would free people to realize their intellectual, physical, and spiritual potential—as the foundation for basic rights of individual citizens. Implicit in this American Dream was a belief in the uniqueness of individuals. Uniqueness (or difference), human potential, and inalienable rights gave meaning to the American Dream.

Perhaps the most powerful implication of the American Dream, however, was that immigrants and native-born Americans alike believed they shared an understanding not only of the concept but of its defining aspects—the promise of freedom and economic opportunity. Both groups invoked the American Dream to justify their actions, to assert their rights, and to challenge themselves and others to greater efforts. In all this, they acted as though the American Dream were a true representation of opportunities existing for everyone in the United States—and, consequently, as though individual freedom and economic security were possible for all who would work hard and behave as good citizens.[2]

This belief in a shared definition of the American Dream hid deep splits along class, gender, ethnic, and racial lines over who had access to economic security and freedom in California in the early twentieth century and over the meaning of the dream itself. This contestation changed the meaning of the American Dream across these splits and over time. The assumption of a universal meaning of the American Dream also hid, repressed, and sometimes erased the very difference and uniqueness of the individuals that it was meant to serve. The economic and social expectations of a brown Mexican field worker in the United States were very different from those of a white American farm owner, and these differing expectations informed the way individuals within these two social categories understood freedom and how it should be protected and preserved.

Freedom, to many Mexican immigrant farm workers, meant being able to achieve economic and social upward mobility by working for wages, putting aside some savings, and opening a small business or going to school, while giving aid to family or community—in both the United States and Mexico. Their response to being prevented from doing any of these things was to organize with fellow workers to protest what they saw as infringements on their fundamental rights. Freedom meant something quite different to white farm owners and operators, who believed that they should be free to hire workers at wages that would allow them to make a profit. Any restriction challenged what they perceived to be their inalienable rights as Americans.

Some of the most violent attacks on individual freedom in

early twentieth-century California resulted from these different interpretations of what "freedom" meant, as did actions that seemed to be directly in opposition to economic self-interest. For example, workers and growers alike often refused to compromise over wage disagreements even if refusal meant losing all they had, and growers (often with the aid of the state) engaged in vigilante activities that included intimidation, violent attacks, and murder.

Competing ideas about freedom also inspired some of the most ingenious and effective strategies of resistance to domination. Contradictory actions and strategies, therefore, become more understandable when we view them within a context of how class, race, ethnic, and gender identity inform definitions of freedom and the American Dream.

Mexican immigrants and their employers believed in an American Dream that promised personal freedom and self-determination, on an ideal based on a construction of personal identity, of selfhood.[3] Stuart Hall's discussion of identity and difference is helpful here in examining tensions between national identities over the legitimacy identity confers. According to Hall, tension arises from two conflicting concepts of identity and from contestation over the content of each: identity as a stable subject—a "true self"—and identity as "a kind of unsettled space." The first concept assumes an ideal self—a model identity—while the second sees identity as a process affected by conditions outside the self, by the unconscious self, and by language.[4]

In early twentieth-century California, two images of who was entitled to the American Dream predominated. For some, the image was very specific: a white, middle-class nonimmigrant male. For others, it was less exclusive and included anyone living and working in the United States, although some kind of commitment to the national community was implied.

The first image normalized identity by assuming an ideal that was marked by gender, race, class, and nation.[5] It was an identity that was preordained and indigenous (in a land where

nonwhite indigenous peoples were excluded from full participation in the dream)—preordained in the sense that a racial
construction of whiteness and a gendered construction of
maleness restricted legitimate access to the American Dream,
and indigenous in that it included only those who were native-
born. There was an implied threat of exclusion and punish-
ment in this image. If one did not embody the ideal, one was
not entitled to the American Dream, and retribution for ap-
propriating resources that legitimately belonged to "real"
Americans was possible, if not probable.[6] Here, to apply
Donna Haraway's analysis of the implications of the process of
normalizing, the physiological and political came together and
provided a justification for "domination based on differences
seen as natural, given, inescapable, and therefore moral."[7]
This image was monolithic in its logic and left no space for
resistance; since there could be only one ideal subject—only
one legitimate identity—there could be no inclusion of different subjects, only a complete destruction and replacement of
the ideal subject. A transformation of the image necessarily
would mirror the image, replacing it with another ideal, with
no room for variety or difference.[8]

The second image, one that included anyone living and
working in the United States, emphasized economic, social,
and political contributions and a sense of entitlement that all
people held in common. It was an identity that might change
in response to internal and external conditions—and consequently might *be changed*, or consciously constructed. As such,
it was a material, rational, and imagined self, in that an American identity was a construction of economic, social, and political activities, ideology, and membership in the imagined
community of America.[9] While the internal logic of this imagined self or selves did allow for the domination of one construct over another, more importantly it also made possible
the development of strategies of resistance to economic and
cultural domination.[10]

Who an individual believed had a legitimate right to the
American Dream informed how one positioned oneself in

relation to others in the United States and the actions that person might take to protect his or her position. Antonio Gramsci's concept of cultural hegemony reveals the ways identity was contested: in nontotalitarian societies, certain ideas and cultural forms predominate over others through a process of contestation for cultural domination.[11] The cultural identities workers and employers constructed were the site of contests over legitimacy, and thus over access to the American Dream. I suggest that cultural identities were the basis for legitimacy—whether one could claim membership in the national community. For example, whether an American of Mexican descent was truly an "American" or was a "Mexican," regardless of citizenship, determined legitimacy. Legitimacy, in turn, defined status and power, and it was status and power that provided the justification and agency for actions taken by Mexican immigrant workers and American employers. The contest over legitimacy was also a struggle for domination—of who would have economic security, who would have freedom. The American Dream in the early twentieth century thus embodied a complex set of ideas about race, ethnicity, gender, class, legitimacy, and domination. In the process of contestation over who was entitled to the American Dream, over legitimacy and cultural hegemony, meanings of not only race, ethnicity, gender, class, legitimacy, and domination, but also of the American Dream itself, changed during these years.

Contestation over identity and meanings of the American Dream shaped immigration, settlement, and return migration of Mexican farm workers in California during the first four decades of the twentieth century. Perceptions of immigrants as male sojourners or settlers and of return migrants as repatriates or expatriates were inextricably linked to ideas about legitimacy and identity, about who could be a settler and who could be a real American and, consequently, about whether return migrants were repatriates or expatriates—sojourners returning home or Americans exiled to a foreign country. Further, the gendered nature of constructions of sojourners as unattached, itinerant men and of settlers as families that included women, men, and children, had a profound impact on the lives of Mexican immigrant women and Mexican American women whose identities were often conflated with that of "family." Women traveling, working, or living alone, or together but without children—that is, outside a narrowly defined construction of family—were extremely vulnerable to exploitation and expulsion.

The following chapters explore these ideas as a way of understanding the complex relationships that shaped the daily lives of Mexican immigrant and Mexican American farm workers in California in the years 1900–1939. The chapters in Part I examine myths and ideals encoded in the American Dream and how the images of farming as a small family affair and of farm workers as migrant "birds of passage" contributed to the creation of an economy and society radically different from both the pastoral ideal of family farmers and the American Dream of freedom through economic opportunity for all. Chapter 1 analyzes industrialization in California agriculture during the late nineteenth and early twentieth centuries and the role played by one expression of the American Dream, the agrarian ideal, in obscuring the industrial nature of farming and of farm labor in California.[12] In Chapter 2, I describe Mexican immigration in the late nineteenth and early twentieth centuries. I explore issues of identity and legitimacy for Mexican immigrants and Mexican Americans by examining farm owners' construction of Mexican immigrants as men who were "birds of passage" who would return to Mexico after a brief stay in the United States. I discuss the ways in which this idea hid the reality of a permanent labor force outside of and separate from mainstream American labor that was made up of women, men, and families of color.

Part II analyzes racialization of the American Dream. Chapter 3 focuses on Mexican immigrant working men and the ways racial segregation limited their economic opportunities in the U.S. It also examines how racial hierarchies shaped the lives of Mexican women, men, and children and restricted their access to housing and education. Chapter 4 looks at the

Great Depression in California, when racial discrimination, the fiction that Mexican immigrant labor was temporary, and an economic depression resulted in the forced expulsion of half a million Mexicans, including both immigrants and Americans, from the United States.

Part III examines the social, economic, and political struggles over national identity after Mexican removal. Chapter 5 analyzes strategies developed by Mexican repatriates and Mexican American exiles in Mexico to survive their expulsion from the United States. In Chapter 6, I examine the response of growers to Mexican repatriation and look at how farm workers challenged the hegemony of farmers by organizing labor unions and engaging in the greatest strike movement in the history of U.S. agriculture up to that time. I also discuss the fears of white American intellectuals and political leaders that events in California, as well as similar episodes in other parts of the country, constituted a threat to American ideals, to the American Dream. I look at how they addressed this threat by carrying out a congressional investigation and introducing Senate Bill 1970, the Oppressive Labor Practices Bill, which discredited both the agrarian ideal as a reflection of California farming and the notion that Mexican agricultural workers were birds of passage. Yet, such constructions of the workplace and of Mexican workers continued to define the experiences of Mexican Americans and Mexican immigrants despite the findings of New Deal reformers. Furthermore, they hid the racialized and gendered nature of the American Dream that structured cultural domination of Mexican Americans and Mexican immigrants in the United States.

PART I

WHITE
AMERICAN DREAMS

1

PASTORAL DREAMS IN CALIFORNIA:
Foreign Workers and the Business of Family Farming

California in the late nineteenth and early twentieth centuries was a place where symbols of hope and renewal abounded. It was a land of sunshine, an agricultural paradise, a western frontier where quick fortunes could be made through exploitation of the land for mineral or agricultural wealth. It was a place where the plentitude of resources seemed to guarantee the realization of the American Dream for all who settled there. It was also a land where the process of industrialization was telescoped, where the transition from small, independent production to large-scale, capitalist enterprise took place rapidly, and, in some instances, where the former stage was skipped altogether. It was also a place where large numbers of immigrants from Asia and from Mexico comprised a low-wage, migratory labor force, the members of which had little hope of ever realizing the American Dream or even of becoming "American."

The American Dream, with its myths, symbols, and ideas, informed the ways in which both immigrants and nonimmigrants in California incorporated immigration into their understanding of the revolutionary economic and social changes taking place throughout the country. For example, the belief that the family farm was the foundation of economic security and individual freedom in America, and therefore of the American Dream, had a powerful impact on the lives of Mexican farm workers in California. Invoked by industrial farmers and their allies, this pastoral ideal gave agricultural employers a great advantage over farm workers. The ideal at once supported and obscured the reality of poor working and living conditions for farm laborers and of conflicts between farm owners and their wage workers over what farm life should entail.[1]

A number of historians have looked at constructions of a mythic American past in order to understand how Americans adjusted to industrialization. These scholars have focused either on agrarianism and republicanism or on the frontier, as process or place, as defining concepts of Americanism.[2] These analyses of republicanism and the frontier myth, as frameworks for understanding industrialization, build on the earlier work of three major interpreters of the pastoral ideal: Leo Marx, Richard Hofstadter, and Henry Nash Smith. Each examined the pastoral ideal as an ideology that became archaic in the face of a new, "modern" industrial world. Smith wrote that a social and economic system based on the "half-mystical" idealization of nature and primitive farming could not meet the needs of a modern technological society. Hofstadter emphasized the irony of the American frontier, which "had been supposed to underwrite the dominion of the yeoman for centuries" but in fact "did as much as anything else to destroy the yeomanlike spirit and replace it with the spirit of the businessman." Marx did not see the spirit destroyed so much as outdated. Marx's skill in identifying and describing the enduring power of the pastoral ideal offers a way of understanding the respective positions of farm owners and workers in American industrial agriculture. Marx showed how the tension between industrialization and agrarianism influenced a number of American writers and painters, who set out to ease the tension by denying "a root contradiction between industrial progress and the older, chaste image of a green Republic" and attempting to reconcile the two productive and social forces. He held that "the resolutions of our pastoral fables are unsatisfactory" and that this is "because the old symbol of reconciliation is obsolete."[3]

I suggest, on the contrary, that the old symbol of the agrarian myth continues to inform how farm production is viewed in America. The agrarian myth facilitated the industrialization of agriculture and the hegemony of farm owners in California by offering a way to reconcile the promise of increased productivity under industrialization and the threat that the republican ideal of a farm-based society of small independent producers would be destroyed in the process.

In California, a pattern of large landholdings characterized agriculture in the Spanish, Mexican, and American periods. In the late nineteenth century, however, California farmers clashed over whether small family farms or large industrial farms would predominate.[4] Large-scale producers won out. They did not, however, discard the pastoral ideal but repeatedly invoked it in describing their place in society and in establishing hegemony in the fields.

Kevin Starr argues that California writers and journalists, such as Edward James Wickson, played a central role in "creating California as the garden of America" and promoting "rural virtue and civility." Wickson, according to Starr, believed that a self-supporting, educated yeomanry might flourish in California and "live amidst beauty."[5] The agrarian myth in California held that the farmer, "freed from the back-breaking ordeal of the New England and Midwestern farm, had time for the finer things. There would be books, a rose garden, a piano in the parlor. Because holdings were small, he [the image was male] would have neighbors, and together they could support a variety of amenities: schools, churches, and concert halls." Starr contrasts this pastoral ideal with the reality of a migrant farm-labor force, the members of which "hardly experienc[ed] a georgic idyll of bourgeois civility on the land, much less Jeffersonian independence."[6]

The image of the family farm in the American mind has

been a powerful idea in the construction of American identity. As Leo Marx wrote three decades ago, "the pastoral ideal has been used to define the meaning of America ever since the age of discovery."[7] The small family farmer as the archetypal agricultural producer also has informed perceptions of labor needs. The agrarian myth had the farm family, along with one or two hired hands, prospering and suffering together. During harvest season, members of the surrounding farm community pitched in to bring in the crop. Farmers hired wage workers only when they needed to supplement the labor of family, hired hands, and neighbors. Thus, wage labor appeared to be incidental and extraordinary rather than central to farm production.

Proletarians had no place in this myth, and so farm workers found themselves outside the mainstream labor market and without legal protection afforded other wage workers in America. The absence of legitimacy restricted the rights and opportunities of farm workers and helped to maintain a reserve army of cheap labor, composed primarily of Mexican immigrants and Mexican Americans.

Those who shared this belief in the family-farm image represented a wide spectrum of the American population. They included farm owners, merchants, newspaper editors, congressional representatives, nonagricultural workers, and farm workers themselves, who often aspired to own their own farms or to move into other occupations. Many saw farm workers as being on leave from or in training for their "real occupations" as farmers, housewives, or students. Agricultural wage work, therefore, became marginalized and undesirable as an occupation at the same time that it came to characterize the bulk of farm labor, particularly in California.

While this attitude toward farm wage labor preserved the notion of an ideal society, the stigma attached to permanent wage work discouraged workers who had other options from taking agricultural jobs. Specialized fruit and vegetable production in California required large numbers of workers for short periods of time.[8] California farmers faced three major problems: first, how to secure enough workers during harvest time; second, how to control labor costs in the face of a short-age of workers; and third, how to prevent a permanent wage-labor force from settling on the land and thus eroding the agrarian ideal.

California fruit and vegetable growers addressed the first problem, that of finding enough workers to harvest their crops, in a variety of ways. From nearby towns and cities, they hired part-time workers who could leave their jobs for a few hours each day. They also employed housewives and school children, who contributed to their families' income by work-ing on farms. In addition, farmers recruited native-born white and black migrant workers, disparagingly referred to as "hoboes" and "bindlestiffs." These were mostly single men who had previously worked in the wheat fields. Farmers learned, however, that they could not find enough part-time farm workers and domestic migrant workers to satisfy their labor needs. Thus, they turned to foreign labor and recruited large numbers of workers from economically distressed coun-tries.

California farm operators addressed the question of how to control labor costs in several ways. By hiring part-time workers, they were able to pay low wages on the grounds that agricultural work merely supplemented other income. Em-ployers justified paying women and children lower wages by arguing that women and children did substandard work and were merely earning "pocket money."[9] The transiency of na-tive-born migrant workers made it difficult for them to de-velop the financial security or organization from which to pressure for higher wages.[10]

In addition, farmers controlled wages by hiring workers from abroad—from countries in western and eastern Europe, Asia, Canada, and Latin America. Many foreign workers ini-tially intended to stay in California only temporarily while they earned enough money to buy land or otherwise better their economic condition in their home country. As a result, they tended to evaluate their wages on the basis of what they could buy at home. Most foreign-born farm workers joined the migrant work force and, as in the case of domestic migrant workers, their transiency restricted their ability to secure higher wages.

Whiteness was the main criteria for successfully moving out of wage labor in the fields and up the "agricultural ladder" into farm tenancy or ownership, especially after the passage of California's Alien Land Law in 1913, which prohibited the ownership of land by those ineligible for citizenship (nonwhites could not become naturalized citizens until 1952).[11] European and Canadian immigrants acquired land or moved into other enterprises within a relatively short period after their arrival. So, California farm owners came to depend primarily on Asian immigrants (who could not become citizens or own land) to harvest their crops in the late nineteenth and early twentieth centuries.

Labor contractors and recruiters played an instrumental role in generating the immigration of all of these groups, particularly in the nineteenth century. Chinese immigration to California began in the late 1840s, when a small number of Chinese merchants entered the state as part of a larger diaspora of 2.5 million who left China for other countries between 1842 and 1939.[12] In the 1850s, Chinese labor contractors recruited workers from their homeland for mining, railroad work, and farm labor.[13] More Chinese came in response to promises of employment made by labor agents sent to China to recruit workers. Most paid for their own passage and were not contract workers.[14]

Of the two-hundred thousand Chinese who came to California in the nineteenth century, between six and seven thousand earned a living in agriculture, and of these, several thousand worked as migrant field hands.[15] California farmers hired Chinese workers in groups to harvest wheat and to work in the developing fruit and vegetable industry.[16] By the 1870s, growers depended primarily on Chinese workers to harvest their crops.

Chinese farmers and farm workers made possible the shift

from wheat to fruit and vegetable production in California by sharing their knowledge of planting, cultivating, and harvesting these crops and by providing invaluable labor and skill in harvesting and packing produce.[17] The *Pacific Rural Press*, in 1893, credited the Chinese with the success of the California fruit and vegetable industry: "The availability of cheap Chinese labor gave the fruit growers hope. They extended their operations and the Chinese proved equal to all that had been expected of them. They became especially clever in the packing of fruit; in fact, the Chinese have become the only considerable body of people who understand how to pack fruit for eastern shipment."[18] In the last quarter of the nineteenth century, the Chinese harvested most of the vegetable, fruit, and sugar-beet crops for large farm owners in California. In addition, Chinese workers did most of the reclamation work in the state, converting swamp land and other marginal acreage to agricultural production. To cultivate the rich Sacramento–San Joaquin Delta area, the Chinese built several hundred miles of levees, although this meant standing and working in disease-infested water.[19]

During the 1870s, more than two thousand Chinese a month arrived in California.[20] After the harvest season, Chinese farm workers moved to towns and cities, where they competed with other groups for jobs. At the same time, economic depression reduced employment opportunities in the state. Native-born white workers complained that the Chinese were competing unfairly by accepting low wages. Angry white workers, nativists, and restrictionists also attacked the Chinese on racial grounds, depicting them as cunning, treacherous, inhuman, and degraded.[21] Anti-Chinese sentiment resulted in mass demonstrations throughout the state in the 1870s demanding an end to Chinese immigration.[22] Agitation centered in San Francisco, where workers and other opponents of Chinese migration organized public demonstrations.[23]

In 1877, the *Pacific Rural Press* reported that farmers were receiving threatening letters about their employment of Chinese workers.[24] The anti-Chinese movement also spread to other areas of the United States and led to the Chinese Exclusion Act of 1882, which prohibited the immigration of skilled and unskilled Chinese laborers for ten years.[25] An 1888 provision extended the act to "all persons of the Chinese race," and the Geary Act of 1892 called for the deportation of Chinese who were in the country illegally.[26]

During the 1880s and 1890s, Chinese farm workers organized a number of strikes for higher wages. Growers found themselves more vulnerable to farm workers' demands because fewer Chinese arrived to replace striking workers.[27] In addition, anti-Chinese agitation continued. Riots broke out in the San Joaquin Valley, around Tulare, Visalia, and Fresno, in 1893. In southern California, rioters forced Chinese farm workers to barricade themselves in packing sheds. Growers in Redlands responded to riots and attacks on their Chinese workers by requesting that the National Guard and two hundred special deputy-sheriffs be called in to bring order to the area.[28] Additional demonstrations took place in Anaheim orange groves and in Vacaville in 1894.[29] As a result, farmers began to realize that Chinese immigrant workers would not continue to fill their need for a large supply of low-wage workers, and they turned to both Japanese and Mexican immigrant workers, concentrating mostly on recruiting Japanese men.[30]

The shift from a Chinese-dominated work force to one in which Japanese workers predominated came slowly. Between 1890 and 1900, the Chinese population in California fell by thirty thousand. Yet, only 10,151 Japanese lived in the state in 1900, and not until 1910 did the number of Japanese in California equal the 1880 Chinese population.[31] During this transitional period, farmers complained that they had been unable to cultivate more than a half million acres of farm land because they lacked sufficient labor.[32]

Between 1900 and 1910, twenty-four thousand Japanese immigrated to California, and sixteen thousand of these worked as agricultural laborers. By 1911, Japanese farm workers dominated field labor on northern California farms and composed one-fifth of farm labor in southern California. Initially, Japanese worked on sugar-beet, rice, and strawberry farms. Eventually though, they worked in nearly every part of the state, harvesting fruit, vegetable, cereal, and sugar-beet crops. The 1911 Senate Committee on Immigration reported that there were thirty thousand Japanese farm workers in California and that the Japanese constituted the most important single group of farm workers in intensive agriculture.[33]

Japanese workers earned lower wages than other groups, including the Chinese. In Santa Clara County, for example, Japanese workers earned 50 cents a day for farm labor in 1894, while white workers made $1.25 to $1.72 a day for the same work.[34] Single men made up the majority of the Japanese farm labor force, although more Japanese women immigrated than Chinese women.[35] The workers provided their own housing, and their employers often did know where they lived. They transported themselves from one farm to another and generally looked out for themselves, placing little burden on their employers.[36] Japanese immigrants organized associations, or mutual-aid societies, to look out for their interests. The associations provided housing, food, and protection to members, while also acting as labor bureaus to coordinate jobs. Japanese farm workers who participated in associations paid dues and a commission to the organization's secretary.[37]

Shortly after their arrival, Japanese farm workers began acquiring land.[38] Some bought farms outright, but most became tenant farmers until they earned enough money to buy land. Once they became farm operators, they tended to hire exclusively Japanese labor. A 1915 study of hiring patterns among Japanese growers found that Japanese workers comprised 96 percent of the 17,784 workers on 1,773 Japanese-owned farms.[39] In the early twentieth century, Japanese workers demanded higher pay rates for farm labor. When Japanese and American growers refused to meet their demands, the Japanese workers went out on strike.

One of the most important strikes in which Japanese farm workers participated was the Oxnard sugar-beet strike of

1903. Japanese and Mexican workers and labor contractors cooperated in a strike involving more than a thousand workers and gained the right to bargain with their employers. As a result of their militancy, Japanese workers succeeded in doubling their wages, and by 1907, they had become the highest paid farm-labor group in the state.[40]

Strikes and militancy fueled anti-Japanese agitation that had been building since the arrival of Japanese farm workers in California. Many growers who resented the increasing militancy of their Japanese workers demanded an end to Japanese immigration. In addition, a number of non-Japanese workers, who resented being underbid for farm work, joined nativists in calling for Japanese immigration restriction. Demands for Japanese exclusion also intensified as Japanese acquired more and more land. Large-scale farmers opposed Japanese land ownership and tenancy because, by becoming farmers, Japanese operators depleted the farm labor force. In addition, both large and small non-Japanese farm owners viewed Japanese farmers as competitors.[41]

Anti-Japanese agitation brought about the Gentlemen's Agreement with Japan in 1907, which barred the entrance of Japanese workers, and the Alien Land Law, a state law passed in California in 1913, which excluded aliens who were ineligible for citizenship (i.e., foreign-born Asians) from land ownership and from leasing land for more than three years. Despite these restrictions, the Japanese population in California continued to increase, although at a slower rate than between 1890 and 1910. Although the Gentlemen's Agreement severely limited the immigration of men, it allowed wives and other relatives to join Japanese men already in the country. Also, Japanese immigrants found loopholes in the Alien Land Law by placing title for land in the name of their American-born children or friends and by continuing to lease land informally.[42]

Farmers, fearful of not having enough workers to harvest their crops and recognizing that recruiting Japanese immigrants was no longer a viable option, turned to other groups to supply their low-wage labor needs.[43] Italian, Portuguese, Armenian, Asian Indian, Korean, Filipino, and Mexican workers joined the remaining Chinese and Japanese in California's fields. A small number of Italian and Portuguese laborers worked on California farms, but many rapidly acquired farms of their own, since under immigration law they were considered white, and therefore the Alien Land Law did not apply to them. Many also moved into higher-paying jobs. Many Armenian immigrants and refugees from genocide in their home country worked as field hands in California, and they too were able to move out of wage work and into farming by acquiring land, especially after a U.S. circuit court determined that they were white and overturned a 1909 federal classification of Armenians as nonwhite Asians.[44] Armenian farmers settled mainly in the Fresno area and concentrated on raisin production.

Asian Indian immigrants were not so fortunate. Between six and seven thousand Asian Indians came to the United States between 1907 and 1917, when Congress prohibited the entrance of nonwhite immigrants.[45] Most Asian Indian farm workers were male; they entered the United States in small groups of three to five by way of Canada, and were experienced in farm labor.[46] They settled mainly along the Pacific Coast, and many labored in fields from central California to the Imperial Valley. They, too, attempted to buy land, but suffered the fate of the Chinese and Japanese. Immigration authorities classified Asian Indians as nonwhite, and provisions of the 1913 state Alien Land Law prohibited them from buying land.

The law also excluded Korean immigrants from the right to own or lease land in California. A thousand Koreans had come to California via Hawaii between 1905 and 1910 to work primarily on railroads and farms; the forty-five Korean women who immigrated during those years worked as domestic and farm workers. Between 1910 and 1917, another thousand Koreans, mostly men, entered the state to work. Some were able to farm land by leasing in the names of their American-born children, but most found even this avenue cut off for them. In an interview, one immigrant, Whang Sa Sun, expressed his disillusionment with the American Dream: "I felt the discrimination and realized that America was not a free country. Everybody did not enjoy liberty. The American people saw the Asian people as a different race."[47] The federal Immigration Act of 1917, barring entry of nonwhites, gave credence to Whang Sa Sun's conclusions. The act quickly reduced the number of Koreans and other Asians, including Asian Indians, in the U.S., since no new immigrants replaced those returning to their home country.[48]

Filipino and Mexican farm workers filled the gap caused by the restriction of East and South Asian immigration. Growers in California used employment agencies to recruit Filipino workers. In 1910, the federal census reported only five Filipinos in California. The number of Filipinos increased to 2,674 in 1920 and to 30,470 in 1930, primarily through immigration.[49] The first farm workers from the Philippines came by way of Hawaii, where they had worked on sugar plantations. Later, Filipino workers emigrated directly from their homeland to California.[50]

Filipinos hired themselves out to farms in groups (or gangs, as growers called them). Each gang elected a boss who made arrangements for wages and living quarters, and had the responsibility of feeding and transporting workers. Many Filipino immigrants had gained experience in labor organizing in Hawaii, which they translated into demands for higher wages and strikes once they were in California. They also moved rapidly into other industries.[51] Although never plentiful in number, Filipino farm workers had a profound impact on labor relations on California farms. Their militancy and organizing expertise provided inspiration and leadership for farm-worker unionizing efforts in California throughout the 1920s and in the early 1930s.[52]

Non-Filipino workers, who competed with Filipinos for jobs, and growers, who were angry over Filipino militancy, joined in agitating for returning Filipinos to their homeland. The *Pacific Rural Press* published articles in 1929 claiming that

Filipinos were "health and racial threats" to the state. Labor unions, such as the California State Federation of Labor, campaigned against Filipino immigration, as they had against the Chinese and Japanese.[53] Because the Philippine Islands were a protectorate of the United States, Filipinos had some of the rights of American nationals, including the right of unobstructed travel to and from the United States. The 1934 passage of the Tydings–McDuffie Act, conferring commonwealth status to the Philippine Islands and clearing the way for independence in 1944, achieved the goal of its supporters in excluding Filipino workers from immigration to the U.S.[54]

A year later, in 1935, Congress passed the Repatriation Act and allotted funds for the passage of any Filipino who wished to return to his or her homeland. Any citizen of the Philippines who took advantage of this offer could not return to the United States. Anti-Filipino growers manipulated government repatriation programs to return troublesome employees to their home country. Growers pressured Filipino workers to leave California under provisions of the 1935 measure, and they succeeded in coercing a number of Filipino farm workers to return to the Philippines.[55]

At the same time that California farmers tried to promote and protect an image of California as a place where farming was a family affair, where neighbors contributed their labor during harvest season as part of a communal project, and where the American Dream held out the promise of land ownership and economic independence, they created an agricultural society in which farming was a business, labor was constituted by an army of migrant and impoverished workers, and access to the American Dream was determined by race. Racial discrimination prevented most Asian immigrants from acquiring land and economic security—from becoming "Americans"—and from undermining the economic and social order of California. Racism also resulted, however, in the loss of a source of cheap labor for growers.

Mexican immigrants seemed to offer a solution to growers' dilemma over how to preserve the American Dream for

"Americans" (whites) and still have a large, cheap labor force to harvest their crops. Federal authorities classified Mexicans as white; therefore, the 1917 prohibition of nonwhite immigration did not apply to them, nor did the Alien Land Law, but the high cost of land after 1917 prevented most Mexican immigrants from buying their own farms. Other means were also used to prevent Mexican immigrants from competing with native-born Americans: racial discrimination, intimidation, deportation, coerced "voluntary" departure, and violence.

Growers proposed that Mexicans be recruited for temporary work and then returned across the border.[56] The proximity of Mexico, they argued, made the return of Mexican immigrants, voluntary or forced, a simple project. After the 1917 ban on nonwhite immigration, growers promoted the idea that Mexican immigrants would not settle permanently in the U.S. even more vigorously, as a way of reassuring those who opposed the recruitment of Mexican farm workers. Mexicans who returned to their home country each year, growers argued, would not change the racial, cultural, or social character of California.[57] Mexicans, growers argued, were "birds of passage." This myth hid a much more complex story of Mexican immigration and settlement in California.

2

MEXICAN
"BIRDS OF PASSAGE":
Representations of Mexicans
as Foreign Sojourners

Mexican immigrants who came to work on California farms in
the decade after 1917 entered a racially diverse work force.
Although East and South Asian immigration had been dras-
tically reduced after the 1917 immigration law barring the entry of nonwhites, many Chinese, Japanese, Filipinos, Koreans,
and Asian Indians who had come earlier continued to work in
the fields. Farm workers also included significant numbers of
European and Canadian immigrants, native-born whites, and
African Americans. As early as 1910, many U.S. employers
had begun expressing their preference for Mexican workers
over other immigrants, as well as over native-born workers,
for seasonal jobs they classified as low skilled. They complained that other national groups made unreasonable demands for higher wages and better working conditions. Mexicans, they claimed, would work cheaply and were "birds of
passage" who would not remain in the U.S. permanently.

Mexicans coming to California after 1917 entered an established population of Mexican immigrants and Mexican Americans who had entered the state before 1917. Furthermore,

since California had been part of Mexico until 1848, many Mexicans saw their travels north into California not as a venture into an unknown foreign land but as a journey into a familiar homeland. They of course knew that they were in a foreign country, but it is likely they also felt a tie to the land and its history. Historical memory, customary practices, and an identification with the land and its people, then, gave legitimacy to their migration northward.

Relatively little is known about Mexican immigration during the nineteenth century after the United States annexed northern Mexico in 1848. Between eighty thousand and one hundred thousand Mexicans suddenly found themselves in the United States as a result of the Treaty of Guadalupe Hidalgo, which ended the 1846–1848 Mexican–United States War.[1] Estimates of how many Mexicans immigrated during the next half century are sketchy. Since the Immigration Bureau primarily monitored immigration by sea and not by land, most immigration from Mexico went unregistered until the early twentieth century.[2] The number of Mexicans entering the U.S. at its seaports was insignificant; these few were primarily members of the middle class who came to settle in the coastal states.[3]

We know much more about the number of Mexicans entering the country in the twentieth century, as immigration authorities turned their attention to ports of entry along the Mexico–U.S. border. Census reports are also more reliable in the twentieth century as indicators of the number of Mexicans entering the U.S. But while census figures suggest the rate of increase of the Mexican-born population and, therefore, of immigration, they reveal only a portion of the migratory movement between the United States and Mexico during the period. Since census enumeration took place early in the spring, census takers did not count the thousands (perhaps hundreds of thousands) of seasonal migrants who returned to Mexico each year during the winter months and hence were absent from the U.S. until harvest season in the late spring or early summer.

More than a million Mexicans made the journey from their

villages and cities to find work in the U.S. in the years between 1910 and 1930. Many came to have a better life—either when they returned to Mexico with savings from their wages or as permanent settlers in the United States. Some came to escape the ravages of revolution and rebellion, while others came because they had lost their land.

The majority of Mexican immigrants who migrated to the United States in the last quarter of the nineteenth century were small farmers. Over 80 percent of Mexico's population in the late nineteenth century worked small parcels of land.[4] During the last three decades of the century, economic, demographic, and social changes in Mexico reduced the ability of these farmers to sustain themselves and their families. The Mexican government under President Porfirio Díaz embarked on a program to convert communal *ejido* lands to private ownership as part of a broader policy to privatize and industrialize agricultural production in the country. Almost as quickly as the government allocated parcels of ejido land to individuals, speculators and other investors bought them up. In many cases, ejido farmers could not produce the documentation necessary to confirm their right to parcels of land, and so they lost the land that they had farmed for generations. Within a short period of time, *ejidatarios* found themselves without access to land and facing starvation. Most became wage workers on land they had formerly owned, or they migrated to other regions of Mexico and to the U.S. At the same time, a period of peace lowered the national mortality rate in Mexico, increasing the population, while the cost of living for Mexicans rose sharply as the country shifted to an export economy.

Changes in land distribution were the most economically devastating to small land owners. Land policies under Díaz forced up to 5 million farmers off their land.[5] Díaz's policies resulted in the sale to speculators of two types of land holdings: public land (owned by the government), and ejido land (owned and farmed cooperatively by communities). In 1883, Díaz enacted a law calling for public lands to be surveyed, subdivided, and sold. By 1892, land companies, through various schemes, had gained ownership of nearly 135 million acres of public land, equal to one-fifth the area of Mexico.[6] One concession of public land in the state of Chihuahua, for example, amounted to more than 30 million acres and went to only seven individuals.[7]

In addition, through two circulars issued in 1889 and 1890, Díaz ordered the immediate division of all ejido land. Ejido farmers by the millions lost their land to speculators and creditors and were forced to sell their labor for wages.[8] By 1910, over ninety-seven percent of all families in the north central states had no land.[9] Small ejido farmers in this area suffered most from Porfirian land policy. So few ejidos remained by 1910 that census takers did not bother to enumerate them, and a pattern of large landholding that had been prevalent even before the breakup of the ejido system became even more entrenched.[10]

Government colonization policies also promoted large landholdings by favoring those buying large parcels of land, which reduced the amount of land available to Mexican farmers. The Porfirian government granted land to colonization companies as a way of encouraging European settlement. To avoid criticism, the government stipulated that colonization companies were to respect the rights of third parties, mainly small farmers, who owned land within a grant. However, since the burden of proof of land ownership within a grant fell on the person claiming to own the land and few small farmers could produce documentation of ownership, many colonization companies acquired land owned by farmers. Land loss resulting from government sale of public and ejido land and distribution of land grants to colonization companies forced millions of farmers into the wage labor force.

Population growth during the last quarter of the nineteenth century further increased the number of wage workers. The population increase was due primarily to a drop in the mortality rate. The Mexican population grew by over fifty percent between 1877 and 1910, from 9.4 million to 15.2 million people, at the same time that nearly thirty percent less land was available for settlement and farming.[11] Many Mexicans found they no longer could acquire enough land on which to subsist, and large numbers responded to labor recruiters' enticements to migrate to cities and towns in other regions of Mexico, as well as to the United States.

Mexican workers not only faced an erosion of their land base but also found it increasingly difficult to make a living wage, as the cost of living steadily rose during the last half of the nineteenth century. Between 1876 and 1903, food prices rose after the Díaz regime stepped up exports of sugar, coffee, and henequen (agave fiber) and shifted land from production of foodstuffs for domestic consumption to production of crops for export. The price of corn, the nation's basic dietary staple, nearly doubled between 1890 and 1908, but wages did not rise during this period, primarily because the wage labor force expanded.[12] Many workers responded by migrating to towns and cities within Mexico and to the U.S.

Most migration originated in the north-central region of Mexico, where large numbers of ejido farmers had lost their land. Some workers found employment in American-owned mines and railroads in northern Mexico, since the Porfirian regime encouraged foreign investment in this area. American-owned firms attracted the growing displaced work force by paying wages that were higher than those paid by Mexican companies (although lower than those they paid their U.S. workers). From the northern border, it was relatively easy for workers to cross into the United States, where they could earn even more.[13]

The growth of the Mexican railroad system in the latter part of the nineteenth century made it easier for large numbers of Mexican workers to travel long distances across the northern desert region and into the United States. Spur lines connected smaller towns to main routes, and by 1890, a transborder railroad system was completed, enabling workers to travel by rail from central Mexico to industrial centers in the United States.[14]

Improved transportation, U.S. binational employment of Mexicans, and deteriorating economic conditions in Mexico gave workers the means, material incentives, and reasons for emigrating. Furthermore, demographic changes in Mexico in the late nineteenth century enlarged the wage labor force and reduced employment opportunities at the same time that industrial development in the U.S. created a demand for large numbers of low-wage workers. Concurrently, economic and political developments in the United States set the stage for large numbers of Mexican workers to enter the country. The industrial growth of the United States after 1865 increased the need for unskilled and semiskilled workers, and millions of immigrants from western and eastern Europe and Asia entered the United States in the decades that followed. Mexican workers took part in this mass population movement into the United States and provided labor for the industrial development of the U.S., and for the Southwest in particular.

The southwestern United States experienced an economic boom in the latter part of the nineteenth century. The major industries in the area—mining, railroads, and intensive agriculture—required large numbers of manual laborers. Several immigrant groups supplied needed labor at different times, but ultimately Mexican migrants filled the majority of low-paying labor positions, as other groups moved into higher paying jobs or were restricted from entering the country. In 1900, the federal census reported 103,393 Mexican-born people in the United States. The Mexican-born population doubled by 1910 and again by 1920. By 1930, there were 641,462 Mexican-born immigrants in the United States, and Mexican immigration had become an important chapter in U.S. immigration history.

Mexican workers in the United States cleared land for agricultural production and harvested cotton and vegetables for export to other states and countries. They also worked in construction gangs, as maintenance-of-way workers on railroads (keeping tracks in repair), and in mines and factories. In addition, Mexicans worked on ranches as *vaqueros* and shepherds.[15]

Social, economic, and political conditions in both Mexico and the United States set the stage for immigration, but organized recruitment by U.S. employers initiated and sustained the movement of Mexican workers northward. Recruitment practices of employers provided the most important impetus for immigration. Recruitment campaigns helped to publicize employment opportunities, and labor contractors helped Mexican workers secure employment before leaving Mexico. Mexican immigrants continued a migration pattern that had been established in the eighteenth and nineteenth centuries, but whereas trade between New Spain and, later, Mexico's northern frontier had provided the economic incentive for migration, now recruitment by U.S. employers for workers for railroads, mines, farms, and other industries both generated and sustained their immigration.

Mexicans came to work in the United States in a variety of ways. Some companies transferred Mexican workers from their Mexican subsidiaries to the United States when they needed workers for their U.S.-based operations. In addition, labor contractors recruited workers in Mexico for U.S. employers. Since the colonial period, American employers had contracted for low-wage labor in foreign countries. During the late nineteenth century, U.S. workers who wanted to end competition from foreign labor, and nativists who wanted to limit immigration from southeastern Europe, agitated for a prohibition of contract labor. This led to the 1885 Contract Labor Law, which outlawed labor recruitment in foreign countries.

The law, however, had little effect on the activities of labor contractors in Mexico until well into the twentieth century. An inadequate number of enforcement officials meant that contractors and employment agencies operated in Mexico with little interference. The law was difficult to administer and, as a result, labor contractors were rarely punished. So, instead of apprehending recruiters, immigration officials concentrated on finding and deporting workers who had accepted offers of work in the U.S. before they had left Mexico.[16]

Individual states attempted to control labor contracting without much greater success than the federal government. In

California, lack of funds made it difficult for officials to enforce the state law prohibiting contract labor and, as a consequence, the statute had virtually no effect on the employment of contract laborers.[17]

While employers generally favored Mexican immigrant workers, other groups opposed them. Labor unions, for example, protested the recruitment of Mexican workers during this period. At a meeting held in the spring of 1910, the local council of the American Federation of Labor (AFL) in El Paso demanded an end to labor competition from those who crossed the Mexican border into the U.S. daily. The council estimated that four to five hundred Mexicans lived in Ciudad Juárez and crossed into El Paso each day to work, and claimed that Mexican day-workers were depressing the job market for American workers. Supervising Inspector Frank W. Berkshire responded that the Immigration Bureau could not prevent legally admissible Mexican laborers from working in El Paso and returning to Juárez each night.[18]

The council took the complaints of its members to the convention of the Texas State Federation of Labor, held at Galveston in April of 1910. Convention participants passed a resolution asking for increased enforcement of the Contract Labor Law. The resolution stated that more than a thousand skilled Mexican workers, including musicians, carpenters, painters, and tinners, were entering the country each month and were competing with American workers for jobs. They further charged that building contractors, railroad agents, and labor agencies recruited border crossers because immigration inspectors were not making "any efforts to stop such undesirable wholesale admission."[19]

State convention leaders presented the resolution to Samuel Gompers, AFL president, who sent a message to the commissioner general of immigration through Frank Morrison, secretary of the union. Morrison wrote that Gompers was "very concerned over the admission of Mexican 'peons' in the United States, specifically by the activities of labor contractors." The commissioner of immigration responded by ordering an investigation of Mexican immigration by land.[20]

Labor contracting, a relatively simple process in the nineteenth century, became more formalized and complex as immigration officials attempted to bring the practice to an end in the early twentieth century. Labor contractors did the actual recruiting, either in Mexico or the United States. During the twentieth century, employers had most often arranged directly with contractors for a supply of workers. However, increased enforcement of the Contract Labor Law in the early twentieth century led most U.S. employers to use intermediaries, such as employment agencies and commissary companies, which operated at U.S. ports of entry instead of within Mexico, as a way of protecting themselves from prosecution (although some employers continued to deal directly with labor contractors). Employment agencies provided workers to United States employers for a fee. They negotiated with labor contractors, to whom they paid commissions or salaries. Commissary companies charged no direct fee for supplying U.S. employers with workers; instead, they obtained the exclusive privilege of selling food and supplies and renting housing to workers.[21]

Both private employment agencies and commissary companies, primarily working for the railroads, sent recruiters into Mexico, where they promised Mexicans jobs and arranged for their transportation to the United States. Employers deducted transportation fees and food expenses from workers' wages and reimbursed employment agencies and commissary companies for their investment. Labor contractors either charged employers a fee for each worker recruited or received a percentage of each worker's wages.

In 1919, Frank R. Stone, an immigration inspector who had conducted an earlier study of Chinese immigration across the Mexican–U.S. border, spent one month collecting data and interviewing employers, employment agents, representatives of commissary companies, immigration inspectors, and Mexican immigrants.[22] Stone attributed the great increase in the volume of Mexican immigration since 1880 to the activities of labor contractors recruiting for railroad companies. Contractors often traveled through Mexican villages on the rear platforms of trains, exhorting *hacienda* workers who gathered at the train depots to travel to the United States. Labor contractors described working conditions and wages in exaggeratedly positive terms and offered to pay transportation costs to the border, usually Juárez, for those willing to emigrate. In addition, contractors paid the bridge toll over the Rio Grande into El Paso. They also instructed immigrants how to respond to questions asked by immigration inspectors at border stations.[23] In the process of recruiting workers, labor contractors publicized employment opportunities existing in the United States, which further stimulated emigration.[24]

Workers from the agricultural districts of Mexico provided nearly the entire supply of railroad track labor processed through El Paso. The majority of these workers came from Michoacán, Jalisco, and Guanajuato, in the north-central region of Mexico. In addition, some immigrants came from the mining and agricultural districts of Zacatecas and Querétaro. The Mexican National Railroad had connected these states to the northern border by the late nineteenth century.

Once workers reached northern Mexico, they were in a better position to cross into the United States. Workers in the Las Esperanzas mines near Piedras Negras, Coahuila, for example, traveled to the U.S. side of the border at Eagle Pass, Texas, to work in Arizona mines. Others who worked near Nuevo Laredo, in the state of Tamaulipas, crossed the Rio Grande into Laredo, Texas, and worked in mines near Laredo. In addition, some miners were able to reach mines in Arizona and New Mexico by agreeing to work for railroad companies. They accepted transportation from the border to points inland and then deserted the railroad for mining jobs that paid higher wages.[25]

Most of the recruited workers came from haciendas ranging in size from ten thousand to one million acres, on which the main crops were wheat, sugar, corn, and beans, and where workers earned wages far below those paid in the U.S. for agricultural labor.[26] In 1900, common Mexican laborers in El Paso earned $1.00 a day compared to the 23 cents they could earn in the interior of Mexico. Seven years later, workers in

Jalisco earned an average daily wage of only 20 cents.[27] In 1910, the average wage throughout Mexico for agricultural workers was about 63 cents a day. In the U.S., workers had the opportunity to earn higher wages than they could in most areas of Mexico. It is little wonder that workers migrated to northern mines where they could earn from $1.25 to $1.50 a day as common laborers and up to $6.00 a day for skilled work.[28] Workers in Texas cotton fields earned $1.00 to $3.00 a day in 1907. In Kansas City, Missouri, section hands earned $1.40 to $1.50 a day.[29] In addition to higher wages, workers could learn new skills in the United States. First thousands, and then hundreds of thousands, migrated north during those years.[30]

By the outbreak of the Mexican Revolution in 1910, few labor contractors traveled to the interior of Mexico to recruit workers. Instead, they concentrated on recruiting workers for specific jobs as they entered the U.S. In addition, labor contractors found that more rigorous enforcement of U.S. contract-labor law by the U.S. Immigration Bureau and of Mexican contract-labor law by Mexican authorities had increased both the risk and the cost of recruiting workers within Mexico.

The Mexican government prohibited labor contracting—not only the contracting of labor to emigrate to the United States, but also the recruiting of labor from one municipality to another, as well as from one state to another. In one instance, Amado Delgado, the mayor of Guanajuato, told Inspector Stone that he had ordered contracted workers removed from trains and labor contractors jailed. To the mayor's dismay, workers simply returned to the train station, purchased tickets to a point outside his jurisdiction, and then proceeded to Ciudad Juárez. Hacienda owners in the north-central states complained that they were experiencing a shortage of labor because of the out-migration of workers. The owners were forced to match wages offered by Mexican railroads in order to keep workers in their employ.

In addition to losing workers to U.S. employers, hacienda

owners had to contend with the dissatisfaction of their remaining workers when emigrants returned with stories of high wages and adventure in northern Mexico and the United States. *Hacendados* reported that "those who have once been in the United States soon become unmanageable and of little use."[31] The Mexican government responded to pleas by hacienda owners in the north-central region by stepping up the enforcement of laws prohibiting labor recruiting from one region of Mexico to another and from Mexico to the U.S. Responding to pressure from Mexican employers, the government, and concerned citizens, newspapers printed articles and notices describing the exploitative treatment Mexican workers received in the United States in an effort to discourage the out-migration of workers.[32]

Their efforts may have persuaded some Mexicans not to emigrate, but they had little effect on the scale of out-migration from the country. Economic conditions in Mexico, networks of information and support among Mexican immigrants who had made the trek north, and continued recruitment by U.S. employers proved to have a much more powerful impact on Mexican workers deciding whether to cross the border into the United States.

Instead of halting their recruitment of Mexican workers through contractors, U.S. employers responded to stepped-up enforcement of U.S. and Mexican immigration laws by devising new strategies to circumvent them. A common practice among U.S. companies employing Mexican immigrants was to promise to rehire employees who left for Mexico should they return to the United States, and to urge workers to bring additional immigrants with them. Inspector Stone collected data for four days in 1910 on immigrants arriving in El Paso and found that of 639 arrivals, 189 (29.5 percent) had been in the United States before. According to Stone, the 189 brought an additional 386 men with them.[33]

The experiences of one returning worker, Delfino García, are instructive. García was twenty-five years old, passed the literacy test given by U.S. immigration officials, had $3.50 in his possession, and, according to the immigration medical examiner, was in good health when he attempted to cross into the U.S. at El Paso. García told immigration authorities that he had worked for the Santa Fe and Topeka Railroad in Stafford, Kansas, for sixteen or seventeen months and that he had returned to Nochestlán, Mexico, for a brief visit to see his wife, Crescencia. The foreman of the railroad company had told García to contact him when he wanted to return to work. García did as he was instructed and received a letter guaranteeing employment for himself and fourteen companions on the Santa Fe and Topeka Railroad in Stafford. In addition, García received free passage for himself to Stafford. The others had to pay their own transportation costs. The foreman, John Sullivan, promised to pay García and his companions $1.25 a day each.

When García attempted to cross the border, he had eight men with him, all from Nochestlán. One, Macedonio Rodríguez, had been in the United States before and had worked for the Santa Fe and Topeka Railroad in Hutchinson, Kansas, for five years. He had left Hutchinson the previous December to visit his family in Nochestlán. At that time, his foreman promised to rehire Rodríguez and instructed him to write when he wanted to return to work.

A second companion, Santana Hernández, twenty-nine years of age, could neither read nor write. Hernández had worked in Morenci, Arizona, from October 1909 to March 1910. He reported that he had learned of the work passes García received from the Santa Fe and Topeka foreman and had asked to accompany García to the United States. In any case, Hernández would have come to the United States, he told immigration officers, whether or not García had agreed to take him along.

A Special Board of Inquiry of the Immigration Bureau at El Paso heard the testimony of García and his companions and allowed García and Rodríguez to enter the United States because García and Rodríguez were returning to jobs they had left temporarily to visit their families in Mexico. The board ruled that the others could not enter the U.S. because contractors in Mexico had promised them jobs in the U.S.[34]

Mexican immigrant workers who were more successful in entering the country, but who were not returning to jobs, were often met by labor recruiters for commissary companies and employment agencies as soon as they exited the Immigration Port of Entry. Commissary companies recruited workers for the railroads in return for exclusive contracts to sell food and supplies to workers. Railroad companies deducted these charges from their employees' wages, and then turned these fees over to the commissary companies.[35]

Labor contractors had offices at all ports of entry, but the major recruiting center was El Paso. Three large commissary companies and four employment agencies supplied labor to railroad and sugar-beet companies. Most agricultural employers, though, did not hire intermediaries to furnish them with workers, since they were able to draw workers away from railroads during harvesting season by offering higher wages. Consequently, labor contractors generally provided workers to railroad companies.

In El Paso, three commissary companies—the Holmes Supply Company, L. H. Manning Company, and the Hanlin Company—recruited workers for the railroads. The Holmes Supply Company supplied workers for the Santa Fe Coast Lines and the Atchison, Topeka, and Santa Fe proper (extending from Albuquerque, New Mexico, to Newton, Kansas). The L. H. Manning Company operated on the Southern Pacific system, from El Paso to San Francisco. In mid-1910, the Holmes, Manning, and Hanlin companies pooled their interests and began operating a joint agency known as the National Labor Supply Company. As part of their contract with the railroads, these companies fed and housed workers on the railroad lines, charging workers for these services instead of charging for recruiting workers. In this way, they were able to circumvent laws prohibiting labor contracting.

The four largest employment agencies in El Paso consisted of the Fall and Mitchell Agency, the Ramón G. González Agency, the Zarate–Avina Company, and the Valles Company. Fall and Mitchell supplied workers to railroad companies headquartered in El Paso and San Antonio. The Ramón G. González Agency, the Zarate–Avina Company, and the Valles Company furnished workers to railroad and commissary companies and received a commission for each worker they recruited. Ramón G. González supplied workers for the Grand Division of the Santa Fe Railroad Company, which operated in Oklahoma and Kansas. The agency also provided laborers for Sharpe and Company and Grant Brothers, two construction companies who contracted with the railroads. Zarate–Avina furnished workers to that part of the Santa Fe Railroad that operated from Emporia, Kansas, to Chicago.[36] Both Zarate–Avina and Fall and Mitchell also furnished workers to contractors for construction work. The various agencies and commissary companies hired labor contractors and paid them on a salary basis.

Competition and hostility along ethnic and racial lines developed among the labor agencies. The three commissary companies and one of the employment agencies run by Anglo Americans told Stone that the Mexican American agencies took advantage of connections they had in Mexico to recruit Mexicans willing to emigrate. They charged González and Zarate–Avina with violating contract-labor law by sending business cards to laborers in Mexico and by providing Mexican workers in the United States with stationery imprinted with company letterhead to use in writing letters to relatives in Mexico. To prove this, the Hanlin, Holmes, and Manning companies hired the Thiel Detective Service to investigate the activities of the Mexican American agencies.[37] Thiel found that González and Zarate–Avina did indeed furnish workers with stationery and cards. In addition, González wrote letters to workers in Mexico in which he described attractive working conditions, although he was careful not to promise work.[38]

However, Inspector Stone also found evidence that Anglo Americans operated their agencies in the same manner. During his investigations inside Mexico, he discovered that the

Hanlin Supply Company had supplied workers with letter-head and business cards. Despite his discovery, Inspector Stone and other members of the Special Board of Inquiry of the Immigration Bureau used the findings of the Thiel Detective Agency to exclude Mexicans recruited by Mexican American agencies on the grounds that they had been recruited in the interior of Mexico. The Board of Inquiry held hearings in El Paso in 1910 to determine whether individuals referred to the board by immigration inspectors should be admitted. In its final decisions, the board consistently excluded immigrants who admitted going through the Mexican American agencies, and allowed entry to nearly all those who had accepted employment through Anglo American agencies.[39]

An example of the Board of Inquiry's discriminatory decisions is the case of Juan Murillo. Murillo arrived in El Paso on May 28, 1910, and requested temporary (six-month) admission to the U.S. He told immigration officials that he had paid his own passage to the border, was not going to join anyone in the United States, and was not a contract laborer. Friends had told Murillo to go to the González Agency when he arrived at El Paso, and he would find work.[40]

Murillo arrived in El Paso with 20 cents in his possession and thirty-three companions, all seeking employment. They stayed at the González Agency boarding house, along with thirty or forty other Mexican immigrants. The González Agency provided his food and sleeping quarters. Murillo stated that he was not paying for room and board, but charges might be taken out of future wages; he did not know with any certainty. González shipped workers out on a first-come-first-served basis, and Murillo had to wait several days before securing employment through the agency.[41]

At a hearing to determine whether or not to admit Murillo and others, immigration officials asked Murillo why he had not sought employment on his own. The officials pointed out that they believed there was an immediate demand for fifteen hundred workers on railroads. "Why is it that you do not have interest enough in your own welfare to take steps to secure employment?" asked Frank Berkshire, chair of the Special Board of Inquiry hearing Murillo's case. Murillo answered that he and his companions had all traveled "together from the same town, and did not want to separate." Murillo could neither read nor write, did not speak English, and was unfamiliar with the U.S. He stayed with his companions and waited for a job promised him by a recommended employment agent rather than seeking work on his own. This seemed irrational to the Board of Inquiry, who denied Murillo admission under section two of the Immigration Act, which prohibited the admission of those likely to become a public charge. The board interpreted Murillo's failure to leave his companions and go out looking for work on his own as evidence that Murillo did not really want to work.

Berkshire, in moving for exclusion, said Murillo displayed "to say the lease (*sic*) a lack of interest in his own behalf in that he never took the trouble to inquire whether labor was to be had at other places in El Paso while the facts are . . . that there is a great deal through other agencies. It appears to me that this alien is a person of limited reasoning powers, to such an extent that he has depended upon others to guide him, and for that reason among others, it appears to me that if any slight reverses were to befall him, he would become a public charge."[42]

In another case, immigration officials at El Paso denied Cirilio Curiél admission when he acknowledged that Ramón González had written to him promising a job on the Santa Fe Railroad. Curiél stated that he had worked for the Santa Fe for nine months in 1909 and produced a recommendation from his foreman attesting that he was "an extra good man." He insisted that González's letter had not influenced his decision to return to the United States. He felt confident that he could secure employment on the Santa Fe Railroad or another railroad with the recommendation his employer had given him. Nevertheless, officials voted to exclude Curiél on the grounds that he violated the Contract Labor Law.[43]

Immigration officials referred an increasing number of

cases for a Board of Inquiry decision after 1908, as part of the Immigration Bureau's effort to reduce labor recruiting in Mexico. The bureau targeted El Paso for stricter enforcement of the Contract Labor Law. As a consequence, Mexican workers, who previously had entered the United States at El Paso, increasingly came by rail through Laredo.[44] The Laredo Immigration Office reported that thirteen thousand Mexican workers, mainly manual laborers, entered Laredo from Mexico during 1909. Agents in Laredo and San Antonio recruited workers for employment on railroads and in agriculture. Some agents charged employers a fee for each worker recruited. Others purchased railroad tickets and sold them, at higher prices than they had paid for them, to workers. Recruiters who worked for employment agencies could earn as much as fifty cents for each laborer they supplied.[45]

Although increased enforcement of the Contract Labor Law brought an end to labor recruitment of Mexican workers in the interior of Mexico, it did little to reduce the scale of Mexican immigration into the U.S. The outbreak of the Mexican Revolution in 1910 sent hundreds of thousands more Mexicans fleeing north into the U.S. to escape the ravages of the war. Migrating workers, immigrants, and refugees from Mexico found that if they were willing to work harder than Anglo Americans, to have a standard of living lower than Anglo Americans, and to not challenge the political, social, or economic standing of Anglo Americans, they could survive in the U.S.

By the time the 1917 Immigration Act was passed, a migration stream of workers from Mexico to the United States was firmly established. Recruitment agents continued to work for railroad companies, growers' cooperatives, mining operations, and other employers of Mexican immigrants. Now, however, their major job was not to locate workers for employers but to distribute them to employers who needed them, when they needed them. Employers could support an immigration law banning the entrance of nonwhites because they had a source of low-wage workers whom immigration authorities classified as white, and who, at any rate, would not remain permanently in the country—or so employers thought.

The large numbers of Mexican immigrants crossing the border into the U.S. continued throughout the 1920s. Despite the end of the military phase of the Mexican Revolution in 1921, violent upheaval continued throughout the 1920s. The Cristero Revolt, a 1926 rebellion against the anti-clerical provisions of Mexico's 1917 Constitution, brought bloodshed to nearly every area of Mexico. The north-central region was especially affected. In putting down the rebellion, government forces laid waste to six thousand square miles in the region. One military leader put more than sixty thousand people in concentration camps in Jalisco and plundered and burned their villages.[46] Three decades of political unrest, economic instability, unemployment, and a high cost of living resulted in great hardship and sometimes starvation for Mexican workers.

Unemployment in Mexico increased during the 1920s, and those who were fortunate enough to have work found that their wages remained stable throughout the decade while prices quadrupled.[47] Industrial workers in Mexico averaged the equivalent of 65 cents to 90 cents a day, yet they could earn a minimum of $1.25 in the United States for factory work and $2.00 for manual work on railroads.[48] In part because of such wage disparities, most Mexican immigrants remained in the Southwest, many of them in California.

By the 1920s, as a result of their dissatisfaction with other foreign laborers, California growers came to rely on Mexican immigrant workers as their major source of labor for industrial agriculture. Mexican immigrants worked in California agriculture throughout the second half of the nineteenth century and the early twentieth century. Immigration that had begun in the nineteenth century gained momentum after 1910, so that Mexicans in California increased from eight percent of the Mexican population of the United States in 1910 to approximately twenty-five percent in 1930.[49] While Mexican workers continued to work in mines, on railroads, and in other industries, an increasing number worked on California farms after 1910.

Between 1910 and 1917, Mexican immigration to California increased at a steady rate. That rate leaped with the 1917 entrance of the United States into World War I, which created a shortage of agricultural labor as African American and Anglo American workers left farms for jobs in war-related industries and military service. Growers turned to Mexican workers to fill their labor needs, and Mexican immigration increased dramatically.[50] Growers were able to persuade the U.S. secretary of labor to exempt Mexican immigrants from the head tax and literacy restrictions of the 1917 Immigration Act, so that they could recruit Mexican workers under a temporary-worker program to satisfy their need for sufficient labor to harvest their crops.[51]

More than seventy-two thousand Mexican workers took part in that program between 1917 and 1921. Most engaged in agricultural work, primarily in the Southwest. A small number worked in other industries. In addition, a large number of Mexican immigrants entered the United States without registering with authorities, in response to reports of war-related labor shortages.[52] The secretary of labor extended the wartime waiver until 1921, primarily because of grower pressure. The temporary-worker program ended when an economic recession led unemployed American workers to protest the employment of Mexican workers, and the secretary of labor responded by rescinding the waiver and ordering the return of all temporary workers.

Temporary workers and other unemployed Mexican immigrant laborers, including seasonal workers returning home for the winter, joined in a mass return migration to Mexico, which lasted approximately six months. However, a 1920 upturn in the United States economy and the promise of employment led to renewed immigration northward, although the temporary-worker program was not reinstated.[53] During the 1920s, the Mexican-born population in California doubled. Many Mexicans seeking to escape the ravages of eleven years of revolutionary war and the 1926 Cristero Revolt responded to the promise of jobs and left for the United States.

By 1920, Mexicans formed the largest single ethnic group among farm workers in California, and during the 1920s they became the mainstay of California large-scale, specialty-crop agriculture. The proximity of the Mexican border provided farmers with a built-in solution to their problem of maintaining a labor system based on temporary immigrants. Mexican workers could return to their home country during the winter and migrate back to the United States when harvesting began again in late spring and early summer, farm owners argued. The possibility of Mexican workers leaving the United States each year also provided a way for farmers to minimize opposition from residents of towns and cities who resented unemployed immigrant farm workers settling in their communities during the winter. In response to expressions of fear that Mexican immigrants would settle permanently, farmers argued that they were "homing pigeons" or "birds of passage" who naturally returned to Mexico each year.

The notion that Mexicans were birds of passage buttressed the concept of an ideal national identity in two ways. First, it assured that Mexicans would not become permanent members of American society and, therefore, would pose little threat to an identity based on a white racial and cultural ideal. Second, the idea that Mexican immigrants were temporary, seasonal workers helped to perpetuate the agrarian ideal of family farm labor. On both counts, the characterization of Mexican immigrants as guest workers hid a very different reality.

While most Mexican immigrants did return to their homeland at one time or another, forty to sixty percent settled in the United States permanently. Those who stayed did so against great odds. The majority of immigrants labored in the fields where they encountered competition for low-paying jobs, seasonal work that provided them with incomes for only part of each year, poor working and living conditions, racial discrimination, and the constant threat of expulsion from the country.

Meanwhile, California farmers, fearful that they would not have enough workers to harvest their crops, consistently over-estimated the number of field hands they needed. In 1918 and 1919, there were more agricultural laborers in California than there were jobs. Nevertheless, farmers succeeded in con-vincing the secretary of labor to extend the wartime waiver of Mexican immigration restriction.[34] There were an estimated one hundred fifty thousand Mexican agricultural workers in California in the 1920s.[55] During the same period, a work force of approximately ninety thousand workers was suffi-cient to harvest California's crops. According to the U.S. De-partment of Agriculture, the supply of agricultural workers exceeded demand throughout the 1920s.[56] Nevertheless, farmers continued throughout the decade to complain of an insufficient supply of workers. The result was low wages for farm workers, who underbid each other in order to get work or who found themselves destitute and willing to work for any amount a farmer offered.

The majority of immigrants entering California from Mex-ico during World War I and the 1920s were male, although women came in increasingly larger numbers in the 1920s. Most planned to return to Mexico after a short period, and many did. A large number repeated this migration pattern annually, becoming the birds of passage growers described, but rather quickly, many of these migrants established homes and communities in California and developed social and fa-milial ties, as well as cultural and political loyalties, to Mexican American communities.

These settlers challenged the notion that Mexicans would never become Americans. Yet, the persistence of the myth that Mexicans were temporary sojourners in the U.S.—for-eigners with tenuous loyalties and ties to their new country—obscured the growth of a low-wage labor force in California, dominated by Mexican immigrants and Mexican Americans and set apart from white workers. Also, the representation of

Mexican immigrants and Mexican Americans as birds of passage hid the existence of a sector of American society deprived of the privileges and responsibilities of national citizenship to which they were entitled. The legitimacy and legal rights of Mexican immigrants and Mexican Americans in the U.S. depended to a great extent upon whether their identity was constructed as American or as Mexican. Perceptions of Mexican immigrants and Mexican Americans as temporary workers in the U.S. placed them outside the legal, political, and social boundaries of the nation and provided a justification for privileging other groups over them. The social construction of Mexican Americans and Mexican immigrants as sojourners rather than permanent members of the national community, however, did not in itself degrade the social, political, and economic position of Mexican Americans and Mexican immigrants in the U.S. in the 1920s and 1930s. Mexican American and Mexican immigrant identity developed out of and interacted with a well-established racial ideology in the U.S. that ranked people and groups according to how white they were.

PART II

RACIAL LIMITATIONS OF
THE AMERICAN DREAM

3

WHITENESS AND ETHNIC IDENTITY: Being Mexican in California

Everyday experiences of Mexican immigrants and Mexican Americans were shaped by widely held perceptions of Mexicans as foreigners, whether they were new immigrants or descendants of Mexicans who had settled in the U.S. fifteen or more generations before. Racial hierarchies in the United States added yet another dimension of complexity to how Mexican immigrants and Mexican Americans were able to negotiate their economic, cultural, and political lives in this country. Employers of Mexican immigrants and Mexican Americans customarily also employed members of other racial and ethnic groups. They hired workers for specific tasks by racial, ethnic, and in many cases, gender identification. They segregated their workers along these lines and often pitted racial and ethnic groups against one another. The language they used to describe their workers became a justification for discriminating against those of particular ethnic and racial groups.

The supervising immigration inspector in El Paso, Frank W. Berkshire, wrote to the commissioner general of immigration in 1910 that employers often spoke of Mexican workers in terms of their "docility and orderly law-abiding habits" and compared them favorably to Greek, Italian, Hungarian, and African American workers.[1] Invariably, employers used similar language to contrast the militance, or expected militance, of workers. J. L. Hibbard of the Santa Fe Coast Lines complained, for example, that Japanese workers were "hard to get along with, very unreliable, and cared little for agreements as to terms of service and wages." Hibbard described an incident in which the railroad company recruited Japanese agricultural workers after harvest season in Fresno and elsewhere in California and sent them to work for the Santa Fe Railroad in Williams, Arizona. As soon as they arrived, according to Hibbard, Japanese workers demanded an increase in wages of five cents per day and threatened to quit by noon that day if employers did not meet their demands. Santa Fe representatives refused to raise their wages, and the Japanese, true to their threat, left "en masse, then and there." Hibbard neglected to mention that these workers would have been working for starvation wages if they had accepted Santa Fe's terms.[2]

In another instance, the Holmes Supply Company expressed its perceptions of the potential militance of different ethnic groups in these terms: Mexican workers "are peaceable and industrious in character," while other groups "are liable to strike upon the least provocation—the Japs especially. Also the Greeks and Italians, if they take a special dislike to a certain foreman, they will threaten him with death."[3] When railroad employers argued that Mexican workers were "more satisfactory" than African Americans, Greeks, Italians, Russians, and Japanese, they were expressing their desire for workers who would accept, without protest, low wages and poor working and living conditions. "Negroes have proven failures" as railroad workers, J. L. Hibbard wrote. "There are not enough to work successfully and they seem unable to adapt themselves to camp life or to living in boxcars," he explained. Although Hibbard claimed not to have much experience with Greek and Italian workers, he wrote that he had employed three hundred at one time at the Valley Division of the Santa Fe Coast Lines and found them "not worth their wages." Although he admitted that such workers were both capable and competent, he was more concerned that they would "do only so much work and could not be driven to greater exertion." He also found Russian workers too demanding and troublesome, "because they always seem to have some new demand to present at the eleventh hour."[4] The reasons employers gave for recruiting and preferring Mexican immigrants had much more to do with whether they believed they could control their workers than with the particular abilities of different racial and ethnic groups.

Consequently, employers consciously segregated workers along racial and ethnic lines and created separate, segmented labor markets to supply them with workers for particular jobs. By the early 1900s, railroad companies reserved skilled, high-wage, and year-round jobs for white workers and drew primarily from a pool of Mexican Americans and Mexican immigrants, as well as African Americans, for low-wage, seasonal, manual labor jobs. In 1913, the *Topeka State Journal* reported that the Santa Fe Railroad had published a pamphlet listing common Spanish words and their English translations, signaling "the official exit of the white man as a common laborer in railroad work." The newspaper reported that the pamphlet was the first of its kind to be used in railroad work. "The white man in railroad track work has disappeared. On the entire Atchison, Topeka, and Santa Fe System only a few gangs of white section men remain. The railroads are retaining their good white men as foremen and roadmasters but few Americans can be found to handle the pick and shovel in the ranks." The writer failed to note that the reasons few "Americans"— meaning European Americans—held manual labor jobs is that railroad companies refused to hire whites, whom they feared would protest seasonal work, low pay, and poor living and working conditions. At any rate, few whites sought jobs that had quickly become identified with Mexicans. Pamphlets directed at Mexican immigrant and Mexican American workers publicized and reinforced an already existing perception among workers that these jobs were "Mexican jobs."[5]

Other railroad companies distributed similar pamphlets as part of a campaign to increase the efficiency of Spanish-speaking workers. These pamphlets were not specifically designed to "Americanize" Mexican workers, but rather to provide both workers and foremen with a specialized knowledge of English and Spanish words and terms that would facilitate worker supervision. The Santa Fe Railroad Company took the lead in sponsoring classes at local YMCA clubs to teach workers English and in publishing an English–Spanish dictionary of railroad terms in pamphlet form for use by supervisors and workers alike. The dictionary first appeared in the *Santa Fe Magazine*, a company employee publication, in order to alert readers that Mexicans constituted "the greater proportion of the construction and maintenance forces on railroads in the southwest." The general manager of the Santa Fe then had the list of translated words enlarged and printed in pamphlet form to be distributed to the engineering and operating departments of the railroad company and to Mexican repair crews.[6] The training dimension of the pamphlets and dictionaries was limited almost exclusively to language acquisition, as employers anticipated that the tenure of Mexican immigrants and Mexican Americans would be temporary or seasonal at best and because the vast majority worked as unskilled, manual laborers.

Railroad employers hired Mexicans primarily to keep existing railroads in repair, although some railroad companies in the Southwest employed Mexican workers to lay rails. For example, the Dillingham Commission reported in 1909 that Mexican laborers had done most of the railroad construction work in New Mexico, Arizona, Nevada, and southern California.[7] Mexican railroad employees, however, worked primarily as "extra gangs"—groups of workers who augmented the more stable (primarily white) work force by moving from one job to another as they were needed. For example, the Santa Fe

Railroad Company first filled section-hand positions with available native-born white workers, most of whom were migrant workers living near the Santa Fe line, and then hired Mexican workers only if any positions remained unfilled. The company hired most Mexican workers to work in extra gangs, assisting section hands in doing repair work. In fact, on the Eastern Grand Division of the Santa Fe system, Mexicans manned nearly all the extra-gang repair crews. Such track repair work paid lower wages than section-hand work and was less secure—once repair crews completed their tasks they moved on.[8]

Mexicans who worked in agriculture had similar experiences, as farmers, too, used racial and ethnic categories to establish separate wage rates for workers they hired. This put different groups in competition with each other and often led to antagonism among workers.[9] In addition to differentiated wage scales, growers racialized tasks they assigned workers. On farms in the Sacramento Delta islands, for example, Chinese farm workers planted potatoes, onions, and asparagus on one island, then moved on to another. Italian workers followed behind, planting barley and beans, with Portuguese farm workers then planting vegetables. Japanese, Asian Indian, Filipino, and Mexican workers also participated in rotation planting, each group being responsible for a different crop.[10]

Similarly, at the ten-thousand-acre Giffen Ranch, located seven miles southwest of Mendota, Anglo, Japanese, Mexican, Filipino, and Armenian farm workers labored in the fields. In addition, Asian Indian farmers worked on seventeen hundred acres that they leased from Wiley B. Giffen, the owner. White workers drove tractors for wages of fifty-five cents per hour. Japanese workers picked melons, while Mexican laborers worked in the cotton field, along with a few Filipinos and native whites. Armenians picked pomegranates.[11]

Since agricultural employers hired only members identified with a single racial or ethnic group to do a particular task, groups competing for the same job often underbid each other. Juan Estrada, vice-president of the Asociación Mutua

Mexicana del Valle Imperial, in El Centro, complained that Filipinos worked for lower wages than Mexican workers. "They work for less in lettuce thinning. When we work for $7 an acre, they will go to the farmer and work for $6.50 or even as low as $5.50." He expressed anger at being undercut and said he and his fellow workers did "not talk much with either Filipinos or Hindus."[12] One Mexican grape picker disliked Filipinos because he had lost a job as a result of underbidding by a group of Filipino workers. He concluded from this experience that "the Filipinos are bad people. They take contracts for less than we do. Two years ago in Imperial Valley they took contracts for thinning lettuce for seven dollars per acre when we were getting more. So the farmers gave the contract to the Filipinos and let us go."[13] H. W. Owen, a dried-fruit producer, claimed that his Spanish (meaning light-skinned Mexican), Mexican, and Filipino workers did not "like each other," and he therefore kept them apart.[14]

Such racial ordering of occupations, along with the relegation of Mexican immigrants and Mexican Americans to low-wage, low-skill, transient, and seasonal work, kept most Mexican workers impoverished, unable to acquire more advanced skills or to use the skills they had, and unable to establish stable lives except at great personal cost. Mexican railroad workers earned a minimum of $1.00 a day in the 1910s and $2.00 daily in the 1920s to keep tracks in good repair. In contrast, skilled workers could earn as much as $5.20 a day in Chicago train yards as machine helpers, but only a few Mexican immigrants succeeded in obtaining such jobs. Positions as foremen, brickworkers, and timekeepers on the Southern Pacific Railroad went to "white employees," according to Earnest M. Clark, manager of the L. H. Manning Company, which supplied workers to the Southern Pacific.[15]

Although the vast majority of Mexican immigrants and Mexican Americans worked in unskilled positions, many were highly skilled. For example, in Argentine (a *barrio* of Kansas City, Kansas), former shopkeepers, artisans, and skilled workers took unskilled jobs when unemployment was high.[16]

On the Santa Fe Railroad, skilled mechanics, carpenters, miners, and drillers worked as track laborers. These workers usually stayed for a short period of time and then moved on to other jobs where they hoped they could use their skills to earn higher wages.[17] In fact, most Mexican workers moved from one job to another, since nearly all the jobs they were able to get on railroads, in mines, and in agriculture were seasonal or temporary. Such transiency was extremely disruptive and costly.

Many workers traveled from Texas and California to Kansas and Colorado during the summer to work on railroad lines that paid high wages to do repair and construction work. During the winter, repair and construction work further north came to a standstill, and workers returned to work on railroad lines in southern California, Arizona, and Texas or returned to Mexico.[18]

In addition to migrating between railroad jobs, many Mexican workers moved to agricultural regions in the U.S. during harvesting season, since this kind of work paid much higher wages than railroad work. For example, sugar-beet farms paid Mexican workers from $3.00 to $4.00 a day during the summer months.[19] Cotton farms paid manual laborers an average of $4.00 a day in Alabama, Arkansas, Mississippi, and Louisiana. In California, cotton pickers earned an average of $6.00 a day, and fruit harvesters could earn from $2.75 to $6.00 a day.[20] Migration expenses, however, strained the financial resources of Mexican workers, and even those who were fortunate enough to find a variety of jobs during the year seldom found enough work to provide the most minimal standard of living for themselves or their families. Few were able to work year-round, even if they worked in a variety of jobs and occupations and migrated in order to find work.

For example, one Mexican farm worker supervised four Mexican families for a Japanese labor contractor on a Fresno-area farm owned by an Armenian. He had no permanent home: "I move, after the grapes, to Imperial Valley for work in planting and thinning lettuce. Then I may work in oranges around Anaheim and Pomona. Then I come to the grapes in Fresno."[21] Moving from crop to crop was expensive. If a worker did not have an automobile, expenses could easily exceed earnings. Most newly arrived immigrants from Mexico worked for the railroads until they were able to save enough money to buy a car or truck.[22] By following the crops, a Mexican farm-worker family might earn enough money to subsist through the summer and cover a portion of expenses for the winter, when employment opportunities for Mexican workers were scarce. Some managed to save money, but at great sacrifice.

Mexican immigrant men and women who had left families in Mexico suffered most from low annual earnings in the U.S., as they sent part of their earnings to their families in Mexico. The rate of exchange between U.S. dollars and Mexican pesos allowed families in Mexico, in most cases, to improve their standard of living, but women and men in the U.S. had less to live on. Thus, it was especially difficult for women and men living alone to establish homes in the U.S. William M. Henry, local manager of the Holmes Supply Company, which recruited workers for the Santa Fe Coast Lines, estimated that only five percent of railroad workers brought their families with them. A much larger proportion of agricultural workers, miners, and industrial workers returned with families and settled, usually near railroads, where they could be readily available for work.

Both railroad and agricultural employers of Mexican immigrants had a powerful influence on settlement patterns, especially since their racialized employment practices extended to housing practices for their workers. Railroad workers generally lived in two types of dwellings: houses provided free of charge by railroad companies, and boxcars owned by commissary companies and rented to workers. Railroad companies supplied houses, constructed of whitewashed railroad ties, primarily to section hands, free of charge.[23] Commissary companies rented boxcars to repair crews. Since most section hands were white and the majority of repair crew workers

were Mexican, racial identification determined both the type
of housing and the cost of housing to which railroad workers
had access. Immigration inspector Frank Stone examined
both tie houses and commissary cars provided for workers on
the Santa Fe and Southern Pacific lines. He limited his evaluation of housing to comparisons between railroad companies
and found housing available to workers of the Southern Pacific to be superior to that provided by the Santa Fe Railroad
Company, but he noted that the Santa Fe was gradually making improvements. Commissary cars on both the Southern
Pacific and Santa Fe lines, in his opinion, were "clean, well
ventilated, and superior to those furnished on most of the
other roads."[24] Stone made no comparison between the two
types of housing, but living in a house, no matter how simply
constructed, must have been better than living in a boxcar
meant for transporting goods across rails. The white-domi-
nated section-hand work force enjoyed better quality dwellings and, in having access to free housing, they also earned an
added wage to their already higher wage scale.[25]

Section hands also had fuel and water supplied by their employers at no charge.[26] Meanwhile, commissary companies
charged repair crews for fuel, water, food, miscellaneous provisions, and the boxcars in which they lived. In addition, each
worker paid an average of ten dollars a month for commissary
privileges. The general superintendent of the Southern Pacific Railroad Company told Stone that he took a personal interest in the prices commissary companies charged workers
and that he regulated those prices, although rarely did he order reductions.[27]

Representatives of commissary companies preferred Mexican workers, since Mexicans spent more on provisions than
did southern Europeans.[28] One commissary company official
reported that "the Japanese generally maintain a mess of their
own, purchasing their provisions under similar conditions as
the Mexicans. The Greeks purchase their provisions and
board themselves, which generally consists of a loaf of bread
and milk if they can get it."[29] The majority of Mexican workers

bought their supplies from the commissary companies, although railroad employers claimed that they did not require workers to do so. As a consequence, Mexican workers spent a large proportion of their wages on food and shelter.[30]

Railroad companies were more egalitarian in their provision of health care to European American and Mexican workers—both received minimal benefits. Companies maintained hospitals for employees through workers' payroll deductions. These were small structures with usually only one doctor to care for workers. Railroad employers sometimes gave disabled workers light work on railroad crossings. When a worker became permanently disabled, the railroad abdicated all responsibility for him other than providing free passage to his home, either in the U.S. or in Mexico.[31]

Mexican agricultural workers seldom had medical care of any kind provided by their employers. In every aspect, their living conditions were far worse than those of railroad workers. Mexican farm workers either lived in employer-owned housing or provided their own shelter, although for a brief period beginning in 1935, a few lived in federally owned and run farm-labor camps. Most employers allowed workers to camp on their land during harvesting and sometimes provided tents or cabins, then evicted workers if they failed to move on after harvesting was over. Usually growers did not provide workers with water or sanitary facilities.

In the years for which the Commission of Immigration and Housing conducted inspections, employer camps ranged from adequate to very bad in the quality of housing provided for workers. Such inspections originated as a result of hearings held to determine the cause of a riot that occurred in Wheatland at the Durst Hop Ranch in 1913. Camps on farms that required large numbers of workers for long seasons of cultivation and harvest generally provided the best housing. Those camps located on farms specializing in the production of peas, tomatoes, prunes, and potatoes, and requiring large numbers of workers for short periods of time, had the worst record with the commission.[32] One employer, prosecuted by the commission for operating an unsanitary camp, declared that once workers "have finished harvesting my crops, I will kick them on the county road. My obligation is ended."[33]

Citrus and sugar-beet farms provided the best housing for their workers. Citrus growers, fearful that they would not be able to secure enough low-wage workers, began building permanent housing for Mexican workers during World War I, when white workers were in scarce supply and farmers were making the transition from Japanese to Mexican labor. A. D. Shamel, the United States Department of Agriculture farm advisor in the Riverside–San Bernardino–Corona area in the late 1910s and 1920s, wrote that "most citrus employers are agreed that, for the present at any rate, the most practical source of additional labor is Mexico. Through the efforts of the American Latin League, and other organizations, the immigration restrictions for Mexican laborers has [*sic*] been so modified that it now seems likely that citrus growers will be able to secure enough labor to care for their orchards, [and] pick, pack and market their crops. The problem of housing these laborers is one that needs the earnest and thoughtful attention of everyone concerned."

Citrus growers requested advice from sugar-beet farmers on the most practical and economic housing for Mexican workers, since sugar-beet companies provided almost year-round work for their employees and already had begun to provide permanent housing.[34] During World War I, citrus and sugar-beet growers experimented with permanent housing for their Mexican farm workers in an attempt to guarantee that an adequate number of skilled workers would be available. The housing projects that citrus and sugar-beet farmers built during this period contrasted sharply with housing for agricultural workers on other farms in California and with housing made available to workers by citrus and sugar-beet farmers after World War I.

In 1918, for example, citrus growers built thirty-six adobe structures on the Chase Plantation in Corona, which housed Mexican families who handled lemons and oranges. Each house consisted of a ten-foot square room and a screened porch that was six-by-ten feet in dimension. The grower also provided barns and other buildings for workers' animals, which included horses and chickens. Chase Plantation packing-shed workers lived in houses made of adobe bricks. Two of the houses had two bedrooms each, with a bathroom between, and included a dining room, parlor, kitchen, screened back porch, and front porch. Two of the houses had four rooms and were twenty-feet square, with screened back and front porches. Growers segregated workers, and so Mexican families lived apart from white workers, most of whom were single men living in dormitories.[35]

On the Sespe Ranch in Ventura, citrus growers provided Mexican workers and their families with land, but the workers had to build their own houses. The owner of the ranch loaned money to those who did not have the funds for construction materials and then deducted ten dollars a month from their wages. Families who left the employ of the Sespe Ranch had the option of selling their equity in the house to another Mexican family or to the owner of the ranch.[36]

One hundred cottages housed five hundred Mexicans in "villages" on the Limoneira Ranch in Santa Paula, located in Ventura County. Each cottage occupied a plot of ground measuring forty-by-one hundred feet. Cottages were eighteen feet by twenty-two feet in dimension and had piped-in water. Some had shower baths. Growers paid $250 to $275 to construct each cottage and provided them rent-free to their workers. The cottages consisted of three rooms; one served as a large combined kitchen, living room, and dining room, and two were smaller bedrooms. Workers did most of their cooking outdoors, although the kitchen contained a stove, dish closet, and water faucet. Native-born white workers with families lived in houses with attached garages for their automobiles, which attests to the higher standard of living white workers were able to achieve.[37]

Following World War I, however, growers abandoned their plans to expand housing projects for Mexican farm workers.

The conclusion of war and increased immigration from Mexico during the 1920s allayed growers' fears of a shortage of low-wage farm labor. Their efforts during the war years to build adequate permanent housing suggest the living conditions Mexican farm workers might have enjoyed if growers had continued to believe that they faced constant labor shortages. Instead, a low standard of farm-worker housing prevailed throughout the 1920s. The housing that workers provided for themselves consisted of makeshift shelters on land owned by growers, automobiles or trailers they parked in rented spaces in employer-owned auto camps, and houses bought on rented land. In the Imperial Valley, workers usually lived in lean-to shacks or tents in "ditch-bank camps," located on the banks of irrigation canals.[38] Housing sometimes consisted only of canvas, or some other material, stretched across branches for sun and wind protection. Permanent camps included a number of these structures, as well as houses made of rough lumber. Many of the camps in the Imperial Valley were squatter camps, set up during the harvest season and abandoned once the season was over. Workers found that growers did not charge rent for the use of land during harvest but imposed a $2.50 monthly fee per family once the season was over.[39]

As in the Imperial Valley, workers in the Fresno area often camped along irrigation canals, which provided water for bathing and for washing clothing and dishes. In one camp, northeast of Fresno, Mexican families camped along an irrigation ditch under a group of eucalyptus trees. The families obtained their drinking water from a well some distance from the camp. Since there were no sanitary facilities, the area was fly infested.[40] Such conditions no doubt discouraged permanent settlement.

Similarly, in September 1928, the Martínez family— mother, father, and five children—lived in a tent under some trees near Clovis, between the highway and the railroad tracks, because their employer provided no housing for seasonal farm workers. Mr. Martínez complained that there were no toilets and that he had to pay fifty cents a week for water to the owner of a boarding house for single workers. He, his wife, and their children had to bathe in an irrigation canal.[41]

Squatters' camps were especially squalid. Workers camped in fields, along river bottoms, on irrigation-ditch banks, and along roadsides. They had no sanitary facilities and usually had to carry their water supply over long distances. Workers either slept out in the open or in tents made of strips of cloth or canvas stretched across branches of a tree or pieces of wood placed in the ground.

The State Relief Administration found that conditions in a squatter camp it inspected in 1936 had changed little from conditions in camps of the previous decade. The camp was situated in the Santa Ana Wash between San Bernardino and Redlands. A group of farm-worker families camped in a one-half-square-mile area and lived in houses made of paper boxes and tin, in automobiles, and in trailers. Another observer described a particular squatter camp as providing the worst type of housing in California. Workers there had to walk to a gasoline station and purchase water at five cents a bucket.[42] The absence of safe drinking water greatly increased the danger of disease in such camps.[43]

Mexican farm workers also lived in auto camps and provided their own shelter in automobiles or trailers. Auto camps often had a grocery store and gasoline station. Since most of the auto camps were designed for short stays, sanitation and health measures typically were grossly inadequate. Employers expected workers to move on at the end of harvest season and had little incentive to improve camp conditions.[44]

Mexican farm workers worked hard to make their temporary shelters livable, and amazingly, despite low wages, a few managed to buy or rent their own property. Some farm workers bought land and built houses on the outskirts of towns and cities, in areas where land prices were low. Others farmed on a share basis, leasing land and paying the owners part of their crop in return for seed and the use of the land. For example, Graciola Camacho, a Mexican immigrant from Sinaloa, worked picking cotton for three years in Seeley. The owner of the cotton farm offered to lease Camacho thirty-three acres of land and Camacho accepted, providing that the owner supplied seed and tools in return for fifty percent of the crop. Camacho eventually leased forty acres, paying his landlord twenty-five percent of his harvest of cotton in return for seed, tools, and water. Since he planned to return to Sinaloa, he did not care to buy land outright.[45]

Other Mexican families managed to buy property. The Martínez family, for instance, owned a five-room house in Whittier, where they lived during the winter. During harvest, Mr. Martínez and his five children all worked picking grapes, while Mrs. Martínez cooked for the family and kept the family's camp area clean. Martínez and his children picked from 300 to 350 boxes of grapes a day, earning up to seven dollars daily.[46] The Martínez family also worked in the citrus industry, picking navel oranges in the spring and valencia oranges in the autumn. The family followed the crops from ranch to ranch, never spending more than four days in one place, and so travel expenses and fees paid to labor contractors strained their resources. The Martínez family paid out five percent of their earnings to a labor contractor in 1928 in return for employment services. During the harvest season, while they followed the crops, they rented their house to other Mexicans, usually newly arrived from Mexico.

Another farm worker, Abraham Chacón, and his family, who picked cantaloupes near Brawley in the Imperial Valley, owned four lots, only one of which was vacant, by 1928. Chacón bought one lot in 1909 for $150. He paid $500 for the second parcel of land and later acquired additional 50-by-150-foot lots. Chacón built a store and nine houses on three of the lots. He and his family lived in two of the houses, and rented five of the seven remaining houses for $5 to $6 each a month.[47] Another Mexican immigrant family who bought property and rented out part of it was the Portillo family. Ricardo Portillo's father came to the Imperial Valley in 1910 from Sonora, Mexico. He worked for a few years, until he was able to buy a house. Later, he built another house out of adobe bricks and rented part of it to a Chinese family for a store. When the store failed and the Chinese family moved out, Portillo moved into the house and rented out the other one. Later, he built more houses and rented them to others.[48]

Often the first houses Mexican workers constructed barely provided them with adequate shelter, but they represented the first efforts of such workers to own their own homes and become part of a community. The State Emergency Relief Administration (SERA) described a farm worker community in Sacramento in 1935 that had changed little since the 1920s. This particular community consisted of 539 households. Residents built their houses out of scrap collected from dump heaps. "The outside appearance of most dwellings is repellant," SERA reported, "decay has rotted scrap construction material, and the overflow piles of sodden junk help prepare the visitor for a sordid look within the household." Thirty-five of the houses had no beds.[49]

The SERA investigators, however, failed to appreciate the almost overwhelming barriers Mexican farm workers encountered in their attempts to provide decent living conditions for themselves. Migration, seasonal work, and low annual income—consequences of the racial segmentation of the labor markets in which Mexican immigrants and Mexican Americans were trapped—made it very difficult for most of these workers to establish homes and stable communities. Gradually, however, Mexican immigrants built, rented, or bought houses in predominantly Mexican neighborhoods on the edges of towns and cities.

Mexican immigrants settled in a variety of places. Migrant workers with families who labored in mines and on railroads lived either in company towns or in barrios of nearby communities. Many immigrants settled in border towns, and a number of immigrants used border towns, such as El Paso, as bases to which they returned after migrating to jobs in other areas. Agricultural workers were especially likely to settle in urban areas in off-seasons if they did not return to Mexico.

Mexican barrios in urban areas grew as Mexican immigrants entered these towns and cities in ever-increasing numbers after 1880. An example was Chihuahuita, the Mexican district in South El Paso. This barrio expanded greatly after 1890. Most male heads of household in Chihuahuita worked as manual laborers on railroads. Lewis Gilbert, a visitor to El Paso in 1900, reported that most Mexican workers in Chihuahuita generally lived in one-to-three-room houses built of adobe mud bricks with dirt floors. Few sanitary facilities existed in the barrio.[50]

Mexican immigrants usually settled in segregated barrios and camps. Within their own communities, Mexican immigrants maintained Mexican customs and established organizations to ease the transition from Mexican to U.S. culture and to protect themselves in a racially hierarchical society that marked them as both permanently foreign and racially inferior. Mexican immigrants overcame great obstacles in order to establish homes and community organizations. They had left Mexico with the belief that they would find jobs and earn high wages in the United States. Many did secure employment, but in unskilled and semiskilled jobs with low status. Workers found that wages that had seemed high in comparison to those in Mexico failed to provide them with more than a subsistence living, if that. Nevertheless, despite their low position in the work force, Mexican immigrants struggled to establish a decent standard of living for themselves and their families.

Some families, after managing to save enough money to buy property, lost their land and houses because of illness, unemployment, or other crises. The family of Fernando Valenzuela, for example, paid cash for a house and two lots in Los Angeles. When one of the children became ill, the family had to sell the property for $2,100 to pay medical bills. After paying their debts, they had only $300 left. In 1928, the father and his five sons were working in a pickle factory in Fresno, while the mother and two sisters remained in Los Angeles. The men planned to pick grapes, do street work, and continue working in the pickle factory until they could save enough money to buy another house.[51]

Low wages, travel expenses, the expectation of return to Mexico, and the fear of deportation kept many Mexican immigrants from buying property.[52] As a result, many rented houses. Monthly rent for a three-bedroom house in Los Angeles could be as high as twenty-five dollars.[53] A number of Mexicans in Los Angeles lived in house courts, which were groups of houses sharing a common yard, toilets, and water facilities. Ten or twenty houses might occupy a 40-by-170-foot lot, with a common area in the center. In 1920, in one house court located in the Plaza area of Los Angeles, residents paid rental fees of six dollars per month for a 300-square-foot house containing two rooms. The fifty-seven people living in nineteen of the twenty-seven houses in the court shared six toilets and ten hydrants with sinks for washing. In 1913, there were 630 such courts in Los Angeles, housing 3,700 Mexicans and members of other immigrant groups.[54]

Most Mexican immigrants and Mexican Americans lived in segregated neighborhoods. They did so partly to be near others with similar cultural practices, but few had a clear choice since racial hostility from white Americans restricted their access to housing. The fear most often expressed by Anglos in California in relation to Mexican immigrants and Mexican Americans was that intermarriage would take place. George P. Clements, manager of the Agricultural Department of the Los Angeles Chamber of Commerce, in arguing against the restriction of Mexicans, tried to alleviate concerns over intermarriage by asserting that "Mexicans don't try to marry white women." At the same time, he played on fears of racial mixture by arguing that the danger was from immigration of racial and ethnic groups other than Mexican: "The Filipinos come over and want to marry the white girls. The Puerto Ricans are octoroons . . . and are often red-haired and freckled and cannot be recognized as Negroes."[55] Edwin B. Tilton, assistant superintendent of schools in San Diego, did not agree, and he expressed the virulence of racial hostility towards Mexicans in these words: "American parents don't want their lily-white daughters rubbing shoulders with the Mexicans with their filthy habits."[56]

Such attitudes affected the self-image and social construction of identity of Mexican immigrants and Mexican Americans. One Mexican immigrant woman stated, "my mother is dark and is sensitive about it, and is always commenting on whether a person is dark or white."[57] Another Mexican woman asked an Americanization teacher in Santa Ana if bleaching cream would make her children white, and another paid five dollars for a jar of bleaching cream in the hope that it would make her children lighter. When the teacher told her students in an English language class that English and Spanish were not very different, a Mexican student "put her fingers on her cheek and said, 'but our skin is different.'"[58]

Segregation and racism affected Mexican immigrants and Mexican Americans in nearly all aspects of their lives. For example, Mexicans had to sit in separate theater sections, usually in the back, in many areas of California in the 1920s. In Santa Barbara during these years, Mexicans and Mexican Americans could not use the public swimming pool located on the beach. The vice-president of the Asociación Mutua Mexicana del Valle Imperial complained of discrimination in El Centro in a restaurant and in a theater, where Mexican immigrants and Mexican Americans had to sit in a segregated balcony area.[59]

While Mexican immigrants often turned to the education of their children as a way to improve their position in American society, this proved especially difficult. Some white communities complained if Mexican immigrant children attended their schools. The owner of the Giffen Ranch, near Mendota, established schools for farm-worker children on his ranch because, as he reported, "the Mendota school people got alarmed lest they be flooded with more Mexican than white children." The grower bused white children on the ranch into Mendota to attend school, while the Mexican children went to ranch schools.[60] Edwin B. Tilton, assistant superintendent of schools in San Diego, told Paul Taylor that he believed the Mexican student to be inferior: "He is inferior; an inferior race, no doubt. The Japs and Chinese shot past him. They are superior. The Mexicans are slow to learn." He claimed that "the Mexicans at Sherman school have bad social habits and are not clean."[61]

Mexican children who lived on citrus farms either went to schools located on the farms or were transported to schools in nearby communities by buses operated at the expense of the grower. Most Mexican children, however, also worked alongside their parents. They attended school for several months during the winter and usually did not go beyond the sixth or seventh grade. Many received only one or two years of schooling. Although parents hoped that their children would be able to move out of agricultural work through education, necessity forced families to enlist the aid of their children during the school year. One Mexican farm worker picking grapes in Fresno told an interviewer in 1928 that he looked forward to the day when his children would be old enough to help him work. "Boys and girls can help pick grapes from about eight years of age on. They can work steadily from about age fifteen. Until about age ten, children are an expense; after that they can help you."[62] A teenaged boy who picked fruit in southern California and lived and went to junior high school in Burbank during the winter did not believe he would attend high school because, as he told an interviewer, "it costs too much money and anyway I have to help my father."[63] Farmworker families required the labor of all able members to survive.

Education for most Mexican children came at great personal and family sacrifice. Luz Romero, a high-school sophomore in Brawley in 1928, planned to go to business school after high school. She worked with her family picking grapes during the summer but had managed to stay in school. In order to achieve her ambition, Luz associated with few friends. Friends, she felt, only wanted to go dancing and have fun. She did not care to marry early, either, because she felt that would prevent her from finishing school.[64] The children of another grape picker went to school in Whittier. The farm worker told an interviewer that his children "like school very much and I like them to go. I do not like to see them do the hard work I have had to do since I was young. I want them to get an education and have nice jobs when they grow up." The family picked grapes near Clovis during the summer and fall, so he planned to send his children to school in Clovis until the grape-picking season was over, although the family would suffer loss of income from the children's labor.[65]

In spite of low wages and transiency, some Mexican immigrants succeeded in establishing homes and sending their children to school. In order to do this, Mexican immigrant agricultural workers endured great hardships and struggled against prejudicial treatment. Yet, low wages, migration, and racism thwarted the attempts of all but a few to advance economically. In a 1928 survey of several Mexican districts in the Los Angeles area, researchers found that the average annual income for a Mexican family in one district was $795; in another, it was between $600 and $800. Since this was a house-to-house survey, researchers did not include the incomes of agricultural workers living in farm camps, whose incomes were far lower.[66]

In an effort to survive life in the United States, immigrants formed clubs and organized social activities, mutual-aid societies, and labor unions. Church-oriented clubs formed the basis for many social activities. *Patria* celebrations, such as Mexico's Independence Day (the 16th of September) also provided immigrants with opportunities to gather socially and to maintain cultural ties with Mexico. In addition, mutual-aid societies provided immigrants with a modicum of protection from the sudden death of family heads, a means for preserving the Spanish language, and other kinds of support.[67] Mutual-aid societies also helped immigrants maintain ties to their homeland. They promoted Mexican issues and causes, and were often supported by Mexican consuls.[68]

Mutual-aid societies also provided a forum for workers' complaints against employers and often negotiated conflicts between workers and employers. Competition and divisions among workers along racial and ethnic lines made it difficult for farm workers to organize to demand better wages and better working and living conditions. Nevertheless, workers, often with the help of mutual-aid societies and Mexican consuls, did come together to form unions, tenuous though they were. El Paso became the site of various strikes between 1911 and 1919. For example, garbage collectors, water-department workers, and park employees in El Paso all went on strike for higher wages and better working conditions.[69] In 1913, 650 Mexican smelter workers went on strike in El Paso. They drew the attention of the Western Federation of Miners and the Central Labor Union of El Paso, both of which supported the strike. Strikers held mass meetings to maintain cohesion among smelter workers and to keep workers informed of the progress of the strike. Employers retaliated by evicting strikers from houses they had rented to them, calling in the Texas Rangers, and bringing in African American strikebreakers. As a result, the strike failed. Nevertheless, Mexican immigrant workers had demonstrated their organizational abilities and showed their willingness to fight exploitative conditions.

Mexican immigrant workers organized unions and strikes in other industries as well. A 1913 strike in Wheatland, California, involving nearly three thousand workers, many of them Mexican, shocked the state and the nation because of the violence exhibited and the deplorable working and living conditions it publicized. The Industrial Workers of the World (IWW) and farm workers on the Durst Ranch organized the strike to protest overrecruiting of workers, appalling sanitation conditions, low wages, and exploitative treatment. The owners of the Durst Ranch, one of the largest employers of farm workers in California, had recruited twenty-eight hundred workers to fill fifteen hundred jobs. As a result, they were able to get workers to accept extremely low wages of 78 cents to $1.00 a day.[70] Not only did the Durst brothers not provide housing for workers (they instead offered tents for rent at 75 cents per week), but they also had only nine toilets for the three thousand workers. Furthermore, the existing water wells were inadequate, and a cousin of the Durst brothers was therefore able to sell workers lemonade at five cents a glass.[71]

The Dursts responded to the strike by sending for the county sheriff, whose arrival along with his deputies set off a riot. The sheriff immediately ordered strikers to leave and fired a shot into the crowd. When the riot ended, four people lay dead. The Dursts and local police demanded that state and federal troops be dispatched to Wheatland, and Governor Hiram Johnson acquiesced. By the time guardsmen arrived, however, most of the workers had fled. Most lost everything they had, little though it was.[72]

Although Mexicans who participated in such strikes against their employers made few material gains, they were able to draw attention to the low wages and poor working conditions endured by California agricultural workers. Shortly after the workers' uprising at Wheatland, the governor of California established the Commission of Immigration and Housing to investigate the conditions that led to the riot.[73] By organizing unions and strikes, farm workers protested their position in an industrial labor system that confined them to low-wage, low-status work and succeeded in calling attention to their situation.

In response to farm workers' efforts to build labor solidarity, employers often called upon immigration authorities to expel troublesome workers. Mexican workers greatly feared deportation. Ernesto Galarza, a labor organizer and historian, reported that "the fear of deportation often takes the proportions of a community psychosis, affecting even those who have legal status as resident aliens."[74] During the 1928 cantaloupe workers' strike in the Imperial Valley, growers and their supporters threatened Mexican laborers with deportation if they did not return to work.[75] Imperial County's district attorney, Elmer Heald, stated that "it would be better if we picked a whole lot of Mexicans and sent them back to Mexico."[76] The secretary of the Brawley Chamber of Commerce told Paul S. Taylor, an economist from the University of California, that a number of Brawley's leading citizens had been able to have the strike organizers deported: "They was [*sic*] three men from Mexico stayed here as organizers whom we deported. We did not like them holding meetings. No, we did not fear violence, but they was going to tie up the cantaloupe industry. Cantaloupes are perishable and we couldn't let them have a strike."[77] Workers, thus intimidated, gave up their strike and returned to work on their employers' terms.[78]

Fear of deportation and the combined power of employers and the state undermined union organizing, and Mexican immigrant farm workers continued to earn low wages throughout the 1920s, requiring all able family members to work. These factors and racial prejudice prevented most Mexican farmworker children from obtaining an education, which would have provided them with skills to enter higher-paying occupations. In addition, low wages forced farm workers to supplement their income by working in other industries between harvests. Perceived competition from Mexican immigrant workers generated resentment among native white workers. As a result, when the country experienced severe economic depression in the 1930s, Mexican immigrant families had few resources and, furthermore, found themselves the objects of agitation for expulsion from the United States.

The Great Depression was a major setback for Americans of Mexican descent. The economic downturn hit individual Mexican Americans especially hard because the majority were employed in the least secure and lowest-paying jobs. Furthermore, the program of forced removal of half a million Mexican immigrants and Mexican Americans, sanctioned by the United States government, caused severe social, cultural, and economic dislocation in Mexican American communities. Many Mexican immigrants and Mexican Americans lost their precarious hold on economic security during the 1930s, not only as a result of a depressed economy, but also because they were forced to sell or give away their property and leave the country. Underlying the economic reasons for the Mexican exodus, however, was the perception of Mexican immigrants and Mexican Americans as temporary foreign workers and their assignment to an inferior racial status in the U.S. Perceptions of Mexican immigrants and Mexican Americans as foreign sojourners and constructions of them as Mexican and not American, compounded by a racial ideology in the U.S. that marked Mexicans as nonwhite and inferior, provided justification for depriving Mexican immigrants and Mexican Americans of their rights and a rationale for expelling them from the country during the 1930s.

4

"MEXICANS GO HOME!":
Mexican Removal Programs during the Great Depression

The 1930s marked the first time in the history of international migration between the U.S. and other countries that the federal government sponsored and supported the mass expulsion of immigrants.[1] Because federal, state, and local authorities refused to recognize that Mexican Americans and Mexican immigrants were permanent members of U.S. society, people of Mexican descent were especially vulnerable to governmental programs to deport and repatriate foreigners as a panacea for economic depression. Consequently, a removal policy that originally was directed at all immigrants became, within a matter of months, one that singled out Mexicans. Mexican removal had devastating effects on the lives of all Mexicans living in the U.S. because, from its inception, the policy constructed both Mexican Americans and Mexican immigrants as foreigners, as "aliens," to be sent back to their home country.

Authorities formulated repatriation programs specifically to expel Mexican men and women who were legal residents and citizens, not male temporary workers in the country illegally, as they claimed. Not only were most repatriates and exiles women, men, and children legally in the country and not "birds of passage," but there is also ample evidence that many had settled permanently in the U.S. By including Mexican Americans in these programs, authorities underlined the widely held belief that Mexican Americans had no legitimate claim to the U.S. as their home country. Although local governments and organizations established programs ostensibly to repatriate Mexicans, the programs made no effort to distinguish between immigrants and U.S.-born Mexicans and, in fact, set numerical goals that included both groups. While organizers claimed that only Mexican immigrants would be removed, officials designed publicity campaigns with the express purpose of spreading fear in Mexican communities as a way of scaring (or "scareheading," as one agency director put it) both Mexican immigrants and Mexican Americans into leaving the country.

Mexican removal began in Los Angeles, where local and county officials initiated a repatriation program to get rid of Mexican families receiving unemployment relief. In his study of these "unwanted Mexicans," Abraham Hoffman describes the steps taken by authorities in Los Angeles to pattern their pilot program on a federal drive to reduce unemployment and bring the country out of economic depression by expelling aliens from the country.[2] Within months, repatriation spread to every region of the country, although most Mexicans left from agricultural counties in the Southwest—half from rural areas of Texas and one-fourth from four agricultural counties in California (Los Angeles, San Bernardino, Riverside, and San Diego).[3]

Growing anxiety over the deepening depression had put pressure on the federal government, as well as on local and state governments, to find ways to ease unemployment. Nearly twelve-and-a-half million workers were unable to find jobs in 1931.[4] During the same year, the Bureau of Immigration deported the largest number of aliens in its history, nearly half of whom were Mexican.[5] The major reason for repatriation given by both Mexican and United States consuls and by returning Mexican immigrants was the economic depression and unemployment in the United States.[6]

The U.S. secretary of labor, William N. Doak, had a simplistic explanation for the depression and an equally simple solution: the country was in economic trouble because U.S. workers were unemployed; workers were unemployed because aliens had taken their jobs; therefore, once aliens were expelled from the country, U.S. workers would find employment, and the depression would end. In 1931, Doak ordered agents of the Bureau of Immigration, which was then under the jurisdiction of the Department of Labor, to locate and deport all aliens illegally in the United States, whom he believed to number over four hundred thousand. Doak's first targets were immigrants involved in labor disputes, for although he had once been president of one of the major railroad unions, Doak had become a vocal opponent of labor strikes since being named to head the Department of Labor. The secretary first directed federal agents to arrest and jail strikers suspected of being aliens. In doing so, agents blatantly disregarded the rights of striking workers, rarely serving warrants when arresting suspected aliens.[7]

The most publicized raid took place in early February 1931, when twenty federal agents and ten New York policemen blocked all exits of a dance being held by the Finnish Workers Education Association in New York City. They demanded each of the thousand guests trapped inside to show proof of citizenship or legal residence. Only eighteen people could not establish their right to be in the United States, and officials immediately sent them to Ellis Island to be deported. When criticized for his methods, Doak expressed his disregard for proper legal procedure: "If you take away dances, homes, missions, and hospitals from us where do you expect we're going to get these fellows to deport?"[8] The National Commission on Law Observance and Enforcement, popularly called the Wickersham Commission, harshly criticized Doak's enforcement of U.S. deportation laws: "in the administration of these laws one agency of the United States government acts as investigator, prosecutor, and judge, with despotic powers. Under the present system, not only is the enforcement of the law handicapped but grave abuses and unnecessary hardships have resulted."[9] Despite the vigor of Doak's campaign to expel aliens, deportation alone did not bring about the mass out-migration of aliens he had anticipated. While the Immigration Bureau expelled more aliens in 1931 than it had in previous years, it deported only 18,142 of the 400,000 illegal aliens Doak claimed were in the country.[10]

County officials in California had much better success in initiating a mass movement of foreign workers out of the United States. Here, too, government agents called upon by county officials to round up suspected aliens disregarded the legal rights of citizens and aliens. A subcommittee of the Los Angeles Bar Association discovered abuses in deportation proceedings in the Los Angeles area that replicated those on the East Coast. Members of the subcommittee found that immigration agents routinely arrested and imprisoned aliens without warrants and documented instances in which federal agents, summoned by county officials, violated the civil liberties of aliens. In one case, agents shot a handcuffed farm worker in the arm because he tried to run away. They had no warrant to arrest the suspected alien and did not issue one until ten days after they had imprisoned him.[11]

Charles P. Visel, director of the Los Angeles Citizens' Committee on Coordination of Unemployment Relief, used similar tactics in organizing the removal of Mexicans from California. Visel relied primarily on the cooperation of local police and federal immigration authorities to conduct deportation raids, and on the intimidation and fear that resulted from these raids, to coerce Mexican immigrants and Mexican Americans into leaving the country. He agreed with Secretary Doak's analysis of the economic depression and believed that California's economic problems could be solved by organizing the mass removal of Mexicans.

On January 6, 1931, Visel sent a telegram to the federal coordinator of unemployment relief, Arthur M. Woods, who was also a member of the President's Emergency Committee

Japanese continued to work in California argriculture despite anti-Japanese campaigns. Dorthea Lange photographed these Japanese workers packing broccoli near Guadalupe, California, in March of 1937. Farm Security Administration photograph courtesy of The Bancroft Library, University of California, Berkeley.

Filipino farm workers brought labor organizing experience and militancy to California farms and played a leading role in agricultural strikes throughout the state during the 1930s. Dorothea Lange took this photograph of Filipino workers cutting lettuce in Salinas, California, in June of 1936. Farm Security Administration photograph courtesy of The Bancroft Library, University of California, Berkeley.

Mexican women working in the fields with their families seldom
received their wages directly. Instead, farm employers paid male
heads of households. In this photograph, a Mexican woman and
man sack peppers near Stockton, California, in November of 1936.
Farm Security Administration photograph courtesy of The Bancroft
Library, University of California, Berkeley.

Mexican farm workers responded to the passage of the National Recovery Act in 1933 by demanding the right to organize and bargain collectively, although the NRA actually excluded agricultural labor. In this photograph of strike headquarters in Corcoran, California, during the 1933 cotton strike, Mexican members of the Cannery & Agricultural Workers Industrial Union invoke the NRA to justify their strike. Ira B. Cross Collection, courtesy of The Bancroft Library, University of California, Berkeley.

Mexican women protested the use of state police power to break the 1933 cotton strike. In this photograph, Mexican women demand relief for striking workers in Pixley, California. Powell Studio Collection, courtesy of the Bancroft Library, University of California, Berkeley.

Employers preferred hiring Mexican women and girls to pack fruit and vegetables, though some men worked in the packing sheds as well. A Farm Security Administration photographer took this picture of Mexican women packing apricots in Brentwood, California, in August of 1938. Farm Security Administration photograph courtesy of the Bancroft Library, University of California, Berkeley.

Truck rides to and from the fields provided Mexican men with opportunities for camaraderie. These farm workers were heading for the melon fields of the Imperial Valley in California. Like the women in Illustration 6, these workers seem well aware of the photographer's presence. Farm Security Administration photograph courtesy of The Bancroft Library, University of California, Berkeley.

The repatriation movement of the 1930s ended when the U.S. government began recruiting braceros in 1942 to provide labor for U.S. farms. Here a Mexican bracero flashes a "V" for "victory" to signal workers' cooperation with the U.S. war effort. Farm Security Administration photograph courtesy of The Bancroft Library, University of California, Berkeley.

for Employment, noting newspaper reports that morning of the secretary of labor's deportation campaign and asking Woods for advice on how to use the same methods to expel the twenty thousand illegal aliens he estimated were in Los Angeles.[12] The following day, Visel wrote to the Crime and Unemployment Committee of the Los Angeles Chamber of Commerce that deportable aliens were committing a crime by being in the United States and that "it would be a great relief to the unemployment situation if some method could be devised to scare these people out of our city."[13]

By January 11, Visel had found a way. He sent a wire to Doak, indicating that he had arranged for immigration agents from San Francisco, San Diego, and Nogales, Arizona, to arrive in Los Angeles ten days later. His plan was, in his words, "to scare many thousand alien deportables out of this district." He went on to urge Doak to telegram Los Angeles district director of immigration, Walter E. Carr, to help expedite deportation proceedings.[14] Doak advised Visel to proceed with the plan as soon as possible and thanked him profusely for his message.[15]

The plan Visel immediately put into operation was to use radio stations and newspapers to announce an impending roundup of Mexican aliens by immigration officials and to publicize the arrest of a few "prominent deportable aliens" by city police and county sheriffs, with the idea of "scareheading," as he put it, or frightening Mexicans into leaving the country. He hoped "an army of aliens would walk out on first publicity actuated by fright and that this would release jobs for unemployed citizens."[16] Visel asked Woods, of the President's Emergency Committee for Employment, for "aggressive cooperation." He reported to Woods that press releases would appear on January 24 in all Los Angeles newspapers, including foreign-language newspapers, and he hoped that they would prompt thousands of aliens to leave the country.[17] Visel acknowledged that many of the deportable aliens at whom he aimed his campaign were Mexican immigrants, but he maintained that no one nationality would be singled out for expulsion. Furthermore, he implied that single men—temporary immigrant workers—were the targets of the campaign to release jobs for "Americans."[18]

Nevertheless, some newspapers carrying the story implied that *all* Mexicans were to be deported.[19] As a result, panic spread throughout Mexican American communities. According to George P. Clements, general manager of the agricultural department of the Los Angeles Chamber of Commerce, many Mexican parents took their children out of school because they believed they would soon be deported. They hoped that by leaving of their own will, they might be able to return once the economy recovered. Formal deportation would make their return illegal, while voluntary departure would allow them to reenter legally.

Others who owned property in Los Angeles called city government offices and the Mexican consulate to try to determine what would happen to their homes and other property if they left the country. Clements noted, in a memorandum to the secretary and general manager of the Los Angeles Chamber of Commerce, A. G. Arnoll, that many Mexicans in the area owned or were buying property, and they now feared that they would not realize anything from their investments should they be forced to leave the United States.[20] Likewise, a report to the secretary of state from Thomas J. Maleady, American vice-consul in Mexico City, mentioned that a number of Mexican property holders in the United States had contacted U.S. citizens in Mexico about the possibility of exchanging land. The proposition, Maleady reported, held interest for some Americans who believed their land might be confiscated by the Mexican government under agrarian-reform laws.[21]

The disingenuousness of Visel's plan to rid the state of illegal immigrants was made apparent in a second strategy he developed. Visel coordinated his campaign with a program instituted by the Los Angeles Department of Public Charities to persuade Mexican immigrant and Mexican American families receiving public funds to repatriate or emigrate. Visel and other county relief officials announced that Los Angeles County would save hundreds of thousands of dollars per month—nearly two-and-a-half million dollars a year—by getting rid of Mexican aliens. Since Mexican immigrants who could not establish their legal status were turned over to immigration officers to be deported at the federal government's expense, county officials were not targeting for repatriation Mexicans illegally in the country but rather Mexican Americans and Mexican immigrants who had a legal right to be in the U.S.

The county also did not direct its efforts at single, temporary immigrant workers but directed them instead at settled immigrants and Mexican Americans, many of whom had established homes and communities in Los Angeles. Officials in Los Angeles, San Bernardino, Riverside, and San Diego seldom informed Mexican families that children born in the U.S. had rights of citizenship and could not be forced to leave the country. Many of those repatriated were under twelve years of age, and undoubtedly some of them had been born in the United States.[22]

In particular, Los Angeles County officials misrepresented those whom they hoped to expel, since in order to achieve the savings they cited they would have to repatriate families on relief headed by both Mexican-descent American citizens and Mexican-born immigrants legally in the country. In 1928, only 2.5 percent of all relief cases were Mexican immigrants, and 22 percent were Mexican Americans.[23] All Mexicans on relief—10,000 people, including 3,248 families—accounted for only 0.5 percent of Los Angeles's 2,270,000 population and only 4 percent of its Mexican population of 250,000.[24] Three years later, in the midst of the Great Depression, the number of Mexican relief cases had not changed very much.[25] If Mexican immigrant families received relief in proportion to their share of total cases, they received $38,000 out of the total $1,509,780 county expenditure for relief in 1928.[26] This figure contrasts sharply with the claim of relief officials that the county would save $200,000 a month, or $2,400,000 a year, by repatriating indigent Mexican immigrants. The officials based these figures on the combined total number of Mexican

Americans and Mexican immigrants receiving relief in the county from all sources (i.e., not only county agencies).

San Diego officials also claimed to be organizing the removal of Mexican foreigners receiving relief, while actually targeting all those of Mexican descent who were on relief rolls. In 1928, 165 Mexican American and Mexican immigrant families received county aid in San Diego County, and officials noted that the number of families receiving relief in 1931 remained about the same. The county spent an average of $61.91 on each Mexican family for the entire year—a total of $10,216.[27] Yet, San Diego County formally repatriated about two thousand Mexicans, over twice the number of Mexican Americans and Mexican immigrants on relief (see Appendix, Table 8).[28] Similarly, the number of repatriates leaving San Bernardino nearly equaled the total number of Mexican immigrants and Mexican Americans receiving assistance from charitable organizations in both San Bernardino and Riverside counties.[29]

Given the economic insecurities of migratory and seasonal work, the low wages, and the prejudice and discrimination directed against Mexican immigrants, it is hardly surprising that some Mexican families, especially farm-worker families, relied on relief to help them survive the winter or to weather other economic crises. More remarkable is the fact that the number of Mexican relief cases was as small as it was. Nevertheless, county officials succeeded in convincing the Los Angeles County Board of Supervisors to allot six thousand dollars in February 1931 to transport the first group of repatriates by train from Los Angeles to Mexico. The officials then set out to convince Mexican American families to leave the country.[30]

The county Department of Charities threatened Mexican families receiving aid with deportation and urged them to leave voluntarily. The county promised to pay their passage to anywhere in Mexico and arranged for the Southern Pacific Railroad to provide special trains to transport them out of the country.[31] In order to gain the cooperation of the Mexican government, county officials promised Mexican consuls in the U.S. that they would not leave repatriates stranded at the Mexican border.

Visel's "scareheading" campaign and pressure from both relief agencies and the Mexican consulate succeeded in convincing hundreds of thousands of Mexicans, both immigrants and citizens, to leave the U.S. The first train of repatriates left Los Angeles on March 23, 1931, on the heels of Visel's deportation crusade.[32] Between March 23, 1931, and April 5, 1934, relief agencies in Los Angeles County shipped 13,332 Mexicans to Mexico.[33] Within a short period of time, officials in counties throughout California and the rest of the U.S. moved to reduce unemployment by expelling Mexicans, using the repatriation program of Los Angeles County as a model.

A total of 3,492 Mexicans left on repatriation trains from San Bernardino between 1931 and 1933, primarily in 1931, at the height of the formal repatriation movement. Of these, only five people were formally deported. Once again, officials failed to limit expulsion to temporary workers living without their families, and, in fact, few men or women traveled alone. Out of a total of 3,487, only 423 were unaccompanied, while over two-thirds of repatriates traveled with their families and almost one-half traveled in family groups of between five and thirteen people, including heads of household (women and men), spouses, children, parents, grandparents, siblings, and other relatives (see Appendix, Tables 5 and 6). Furthermore, many were young children (over 40 percent were under twelve years of age), and it is likely that a large proportion of these were born in the U.S. (Table 7).[34]

The first group of Mexican repatriates left San Bernardino on April 22, 1931. One woman and twenty-three men traveling alone, in addition to sixty-two family groups, traveled by Southern Pacific Railroad to Ciudad Juárez, where they transferred to Mexican National Railroad trains for their journey to their final destinations.[35] On May 10, the second train carrying repatriates left San Bernardino with sixty-seven families and another thirteen men and women on board. The majority traveled to towns and villages in north-central Mexican states, such as Durango, Guanajuato, Jalisco, and Michoacán.[36]

The Mexican government worked closely with U.S. officials in organizing and carrying out repatriation programs in San Bernardino and other cities around the country. Mexican leaders had been deeply troubled by the large numbers of workers leaving Mexico in the early years of the twentieth century, especially since proponents of Mexican industrialization viewed the loss of labor through emigration as a threat to industrial development and growth. Large-scale emigration had proven especially embarrassing since the Mexican Revolution had been dedicated to eliminating the economic inequities that prompted Mexican workers to leave the country.[37]

As a result, Mexican consuls in California and other states cooperated with local officials in a number of ways. They helped to locate and identify Mexicans who might be convinced to leave the U.S. In addition, the Mexican government helped defray repatriation costs by paying for travel from the U.S.–Mexican border to places in the interior where repatriates wanted to settle. In some instances, Mexican consuls also ran repatriation programs for U.S. county agencies.

In San Bernardino, for example, the Mexican consulate coordinated the repatriation of Mexicans from San Bernardino and Riverside counties. The San Bernardino consulate helped to repatriate Mexican farm workers on relief and Mexican families who had exhausted their financial resources in both Riverside and San Bernardino counties. San Bernardino and Riverside counties and the Comité Mexicano de Beneficiencia paid the fares of the first five groups of repatriates leaving the area.[38] On June 21, 1931, the Riverside County Charity Department voted to pay the passage of another 150 indigent Mexican families (approximately 750 people) to El Paso. A month later, the county raised the number to 200 families.[39] These families departed by train from nearby San Bernardino on July 22.[40]

The Mexican government agreed to pay passage to final

destination points for this and all subsequent groups. The first trains carrying repatriates left San Bernardino in April 1931.[41] After that, trains left San Bernardino on an average of one per month until February 1933. Each train carried from 150 to 400 repatriates and their belongings. The trains went either to Ciudad Juárez or Nogales, where repatriates disembarked. A few remained at the border and attempted to find work, but most continued on to points in the interior of Mexico. Mexican officials made arrangements to send repatriates to the regions from which they originated, with the idea that friends and relatives might help repatriates to settle and find employment.[42]

The Mexican consulate also coordinated the repatriation of indigent Mexicans from San Diego County, with the help of local charitable organizations. The Mexican consul arranged for transportation of Mexicans who requested help or who were persuaded by relief-agency personnel to leave the U.S., although the number of Mexican families receiving relief was relatively small. Enrique Ferreira, Mexican consul in San Diego, reported in early April 1931 that relief agencies were pressuring Mexican immigrants to return to Mexico and that, as a consequence, many Mexican immigrants had appealed to him for financial assistance for the return trip. The majority, Ferreira wrote, were of the working class; many had not been able to find jobs for the previous four or five months and thus lacked resources to pay for their passage. Ferreira pointed out that he was aware that the Mexican government had helped others return, and he hoped that Mexico would come to the aid of these families as well. In closing, Consul Ferreira asked for government reports on the repatriation program that had been organized in Los Angeles, so that he could be better able to advise Mexicans in San Diego.[43]

In June, Ferreira contacted the Mexican government again, this time to ask that the government help reduce repatriates' relocation costs by waiving the ten-peso Certificate of Residence fee the government required of all nonresidents entering the country. The Mexican government evidently gave high priority to repatriation: The secretariat of foreign relations responded immediately to Ferreira, with an airmail letter marked "urgent," that the matter would be resolved within a few days and that Ferreira would be notified by telegram of the government's decision.[44] The director of the secretariat of finance notified him ten days later that the fee would be waived for repatriates.[45]

The following month, Ferreira reported to the secretariat of foreign relations that the San Diego County Welfare Commission had requested that the Mexican government contribute to the expense of repatriating indigent Mexicans. The county representative, Arthur M. Louch, told Ferreira that the commission wanted to repatriate Mexicans, especially those who had been receiving relief for several years. Louch emphasized that the county would not try to force Mexicans to leave, but he feared Mexicans would have a more difficult time than others in recovering from the depression and did not want them to be a burden on their relief program for years to come.[46] Ferreira was able to give Mexican officials detailed information about how many Mexican families might be repatriated, what the costs would be, and how many cars would be needed from the Southern Pacific, the Santa Fe, and the San Diego and Arizona railroads because the commission had sponsored a study to determine which Mexican families could be convinced to leave the country.[47]

Private transportation companies also cooperated with the Mexican government and local relief agencies to expel Mexicans. They lowered rail fares for Mexican repatriates and applied to the federal government to waive price restrictions on fares. For example, on August 10, 1931, Louch and L. D. Carrol, an agent of the Southern Pacific lines, visited Consul Ferreira in San Diego to report that the project to repatriate indigent Mexicans had been approved by the company and the federal government. A train carrying the first group of thirty-five families would leave the following week. Ferreira urged the Mexican government to provide any aid it could to repatriates because many of the families scheduled to leave in this group had visited him asking for help and were "in a truly difficult economic situation."[48] On August 16, formal repatriation from San Diego began. The thirty-five families from San Diego traveled to Nilan, in Imperial County, where they were joined by a group of repatriates from Los Angeles County. The next group left in October.[49]

About two thousand Mexicans took part in formal repatriation from San Diego.[50] Almost half (928) went to Baja California, and over 70 percent went to the border states of Baja California, Sinaloa, Sonora, Chihuahua, and Coahuila. Only 15 percent went to the north-central states of Durango, Jalisco, Michoacán, Guanajuato, and Zacatecas (see Appendix, Table 4). The San Diego County Welfare Commission planned to repatriate more Mexicans in 1932 but wanted assurance that the Mexican government would continue to pay passage to interior destination points.

Armando C. Amador, Mexican consul in San Diego in 1932, devised a plan that would reduce the expense of transporting repatriates south. On March 4, 1932, Amador attended a luncheon for officers of a Mexican warship, the *Progreso*. The same day, Amador informed the Mexican ambassador in Washington that the warship would be taking eight hundred repatriates to Topolobampo, Sinaloa. The passengers would then continue to the interior by rail. Amador had apparently neglected to obtain official approval from the secretariat to use the ship to transport repatriates, because on March 17 he sent an airgram to the secretariat of foreign relations suggesting the idea of using the *Progreso* to repatriate indigent Mexicans. He pointed out that the warship could carry eight hundred passengers at a cost of sixty cents in gold per day (480 pesos). He estimated it would take ten days for the ship to arrive at its destination, so that the cost would be $2,400 for feeding passengers, plus another $2,400 for fuel. Los Angeles, he reported, could provide six hundred passengers, while there were two hundred waiting for transportation in San Diego. He concluded by urging the secretariat to notify him if his plan was approved.[51]

The Mexican government approved Amador's plan, but it was not until August that it was put into motion. The government offered land in any one of six states (Sonora, Sinaloa, Nayarit, Jalisco, Michoacán, or Guanajuato) to repatriates who would travel aboard the *Progreso*, to help repatriates in getting established in Mexico.[52] Prospective passengers filled out a form indicating the name, address, age, occupation, and place of birth of the head of household, and the names, ages, and relationships of those accompanying him or her; they also indicated on the form which of the six states would be their destination.[53]

Although a number of people had initially agreed to travel on the warship, few actually did. Amador felt this was because many were afraid of traveling by sea. Others boarded the ship before it was ready to leave, only to find that no one had prepared accommodations for passengers and that sanitary conditions were poor. Many of these people left the ship without notifying authorities. Some, including a number of Mexican Americans, changed their minds at the last minute about leaving, in the hope that economic conditions would improve. Amador reported that he did not know exactly how many people actually sailed on the *Progreso*, but he estimated that there were fewer than 250.[54]

In addition to directing repatriation, the Mexican government took the initiative in a number of other ways. For example, the Mexican departments of transportation, customs, and sanitation coordinated programs to care for and transport large numbers of people to the interior. In one instance, eight repatriates suffering from serious diseases (tuberculosis and syphilis) arrived at Ciudad Juárez. Mexican health officials met them at the Ciudad Juárez train depot and attended to them.[55] Mexican authorities also responded to repatriates' requests for financial assistance. The Mexican consul in San Bernardino, Fernando Alatorre, referred indigent Mexicans to the county for repatriation and arranged for financial assistance for them in the interim.

In one case, the consular department in Mexico City directed the Mexican consul in Los Angeles to arrange for the repatriation of Refugio García de Morales, a widow with four children. The department mentioned that García's sister, Altagracia García of Mexico City, had notified officials that she had found her sister in "an anguished condition" over her lack of resources to pay the cost of traveling to Mexico City to join her family.[56] The secretariat of foreign relations recommended that the consul secure the help of American authorities or charitable societies. The consul moved quickly to help García and, on January 28, the secretariat received word that arrangements had been made for the departure of García and her family. García, the consul had learned, lived in San Bernardino County. He notified Consul Alatorre of the secretariat's recommendations, and Alatorre arranged for García to leave San Bernardino on February 2 aboard a repatriation train to Ciudad Juárez, from whence she and her children would continue to Mexico City. Her passage was to be paid by the Mexican Department of Migration.[57]

The Mexican government also helped repatriates transport their belongings. Many of the repatriates had owned their own homes and had decided to settle in the U.S. The list of belongings repatriates transported to Mexico when they left the U.S., therefore, included a wide variety of articles: sewing machines, radios, typewriters, beds and mattresses, wheelchairs, books, baby carriages, bicycles, and rifles. Some travelers found, to their dismay, that they had exceeded the weight allowed for baggage and were forced to leave some of their belongings behind. The Mexican consul in San Bernardino reported this problem to his superiors in Mexico City, and the government responded by ordering the Mexican National Railroad to increase the excess-baggage allowance for passengers from the Mexican border to destination points in the interior.[58]

In an individual case, a passenger on the *Progreso*, Jimeno Hernández, fourteen years of age, wrote a letter to his family's former landlady, Mrs. S. F. Holcomb, Jr., in San Diego, asking for help in arranging for their belongings to be transported to

Mexico. He wrote that he, his seven brothers and sisters, his mother, and his father had left aboard the *Progreso* in late August 1932. Although the trip had been a pleasant one, problems arose upon landing in Manzanillo, where Mexican immigration authorities informed the family that their baggage exceeded the allowed weight. They were allowed 150 pounds of baggage free for each ticket. They had four full-fare and four half fare tickets, but their belongings weighed more than the 900 pounds allowed. Authorities told Jimeno's father that he owed 111 pesos (37 dollars). He did not have this sum and, as a result, the family was forced to leave behind their sewing machine, Jimeno's typewriter and bicycle, the family's beds, and the tools Jimeno's father had taken with him.[59] Holcomb responded by reporting the loss of these belongings to the Mexican consul in San Diego. In her letter to the consul, she mentioned that the Hernández family had been her tenants for many years in San Diego and that she hoped the consulate would be able to help the family. The consul relayed the information and copies of letters from Hernández and Holcomb to authorities in Mexico City.[60] There is no record of how the problem was resolved, but the correspondence reveals the vulnerability of this repatriate family and how wrenching their dislocation must have been. It also reveals the close relationship that had developed between the Hernández family and their landlady—one in which paternalistic benevolence could be turned to the Mexican family's advantage.

Repatriation and the atmosphere of hostility and fear that it created devastated the lives of Mexicans in California. Many who had succeeded against great odds in buying property, placing their children in schools, and establishing stable communities lost all they had worked for during the repatriation drive. Mexican Americans and Mexican immigrants in other regions in the U.S. suffered similarly. County welfare agencies around the country learned of the repatriation drives in California and instituted programs of their own to expel Mexican American and Mexican immigrant families in economic distress. For example, Paul S. Taylor, a leading expert on Mexican immigration, estimated that 18,520 Mexicans (over 16 percent of the state's 1930 Mexican population) were repatriated from Arizona between 1930 and 1932.[61] An estimated 1,800 left East Chicago, Indiana, in 1932, and another 1,500 were repatriated from Gary, Indiana.[62]

Mexican consulates in at least ten states corresponded with the secretariat of foreign affairs in Mexico City about repatriation programs being planned or under way in their jurisdictions. Cities represented in this correspondence include New Orleans; New York; Boston; Salt Lake City; Oklahoma City; Laredo, Texas; Fresno, California; and Bisbee, Arizona. In Detroit, the Pro-Repatriation Committee requested the repatriation of Mexican families in 1932.[63] That same year, the consulate in Fresno reported to the secretariat concerning repatriates who had left the area. The consulates in Galveston, Texas, and New York City both submitted reports about repatriates who had traveled to Mexico on ships owned by the American Fruit and Steamship Corporation and the Compañía Mexicana de Petróleo.[64]

In Nuevo Laredo, Tamaulipas, along the Mexican border, four to five hundred repatriates gathered at the customs house, in waiting rooms and corridors, in front of the migration office, and in other public places hoping for transportation and assistance to go to the interior. The migration authorities at Nuevo Laredo contacted the Mexican secretary of state requesting that the Mexican National Railway provide one or two cars to take these people to their final destinations.[65] Repatriation via Nuevo Laredo continued through 1931 and 1932. In 1931, 47,314 passed through Nuevo Laredo. Another 25,939 left the United States through this border station the following year. Several trainloads of destitute, unemployed Mexicans from Chicago, Detroit, Gary, and other eastern and midwestern cities entered Nuevo Laredo on their way to the interior of Mexico in 1932.[66]

During 1931, 35,417 repatriates entered Mexico through Ciudad Juárez by rail, by automobile, and on foot. Nearly all went to the interior, to areas they had listed as places of origin when they registered with the Mexican Migration Service. By the end of 1931, only five hundred repatriates remained in Ciudad Juárez. Most were able to support themselves without government aid, according to the United States consul there, and so would be allowed to remain.[67]

Repatriation began to slow after 1932. In all, more than three hundred and sixty-five thousand Mexican immigrants and Mexican Americans left the United States for Mexico between 1929 and 1932. U.S. authorities, though, did not simply "return" Mexicans to their home country, but sent many American citizens into exile in a foreign country. Repatriation and exile continued to shape the experiences of Mexican Americans and Mexican immigrants in both the U.S. and Mexico for generations.

PART III
DREAMING AMERICA

5

LOS REPATRIADOS:
America's Exiles in Mexico

Many Mexican immigrants and Mexican Americans who left the United States hoping that they would find a homeland—a place where they could escape the discrimination and racial oppression that repatriation symbolized—discovered that Mexico was not the refuge they had hoped it would be. Others, who had experienced repatriation as exile, indeed felt themselves to be exiles once relocated in Mexico. A smaller number happily abandoned the American Dream for life in a country where they were not considered perpetual foreigners.

Repatriation exposed the racial limitations of the American Dream for Mexican Americans, who found that they were considered foreign in the U.S. no matter how many generations they had lived in the country. It brought about a crisis of identity and legitimacy for Mexican Americans, which left a profound legacy for later generations of Mexicans and Mexican Americans alike. Narratives about repatriation circulated in both the U.S. and Mexico and were passed on to children, destabilizing ideas about the American Dream and the possibility of transplanted Mexicans ever acquiring an American identity. Compounding this, Mexican American repatriates found they were often considered foreign in Mexico as well—*pochos* who were somewhere between Mexican and American, illegitimate in both cultures.

Besides revealing the ways in which the American Dream was racialized, repatriation also demonstrated the consequences for women of a construction of Mexican immigrants as "birds of passage," a construction that was gendered as male in every instance. The argument that Mexican immigrants were birds of passage—temporary male workers—provided the legal justification for establishing repatriation programs, but relief agencies were able to use these programs to expel all Mexicans, including women. In the official rhetoric of repatriation—indeed, in the language of farm-labor recruitment and employment—women were largely invisible. Ironically, repatriated women in Mexico discovered that Mexicans saw them as spoiled by their American experience, as pochos of the worst sort. Women and men alike faced crises of identity and legitimacy as a result of repatriation, but sometimes these were crises of different sorts.

When they arrived in Mexico, both repatriated women and repatriated men found themselves in economic trouble. The large numbers of repatriates and the absence of effective coordination of their relocation within Mexico made the transition for most of them extremely difficult. While the U.S. and Mexican governments had often cooperated in carrying out formal repatriation, they had little control over the flood of Mexican Americans and Mexican immigrants fleeing the U.S. on their own because they feared deportation or starvation. Mexican women, men, and children who took part in formal repatriation programs joined a stream of returning immigrants who could not establish that they were in the U.S. legally. In 1929, seventy-nine thousand Mexicans returned to Mexico. Another seventy thousand left in 1930. The largest number, one hundred twenty-five thousand, left for Mexico in 1931, including seventy-six thousand men and forty-nine thousand women, according to statistics gathered by the Mexican Migration Service.[1]

Richard P. Boyce, the American consul in Nuevo León, Mexico, had reported to the United States secretary of state in

late 1930 that thousands of Mexican residents of the United
States were returning to Mexico through Laredo: "In crossing
the international bridge each day one can always see a line of
cars with licenses from nearly half the states of the United
States filled with household effects of Mexicans returning and
waiting to make the necessary registrations with the Mexican
authorities." Most of the cars, Boyce wrote, were dilapidated
and showed the effects of the long journey from the northern
sections of the country. Yet, only half the repatriates had automobiles; the other half walked across the border. In October,
4,255 repatriates crossed the border. Another 3,995 crossed
in the first twenty-four days of November. According to
Boyce, "quite a number" of the Mexicans returning had lived
in the United States for more than five years. Some claimed to
have been there eight, ten, fifteen, and even thirty years.[2]

Boyce estimated that eighty percent were returning because
of lack of work in the United States. He quoted one Mexican,
coming from a Colorado settlement with a Mexican population of one thousand, as saying that nearly the entire community was returning to Mexico because of unemployment. Some
were headed for the Don Martín irrigation project in Nuevo
León, having read advertisements issued by the Mexican government offering land to repatriates there.[3]

Most of these repatriates, Boyce believed, had been in the
U.S. illegally. He came to this conclusion because he learned
from the Mexican Migration Service that many *repatriados* had
applied for entrance visas. Since it was against Mexican law for
anyone, even a citizen, to enter Mexico without registering
with that country's authorities, most returning migrants did
register. He concluded that those applying for visas had not
registered with immigration authorities when they left Mexico, because if they had, they would have been able to reenter
Mexico within a six-month period without visas. He failed to
consider that these immigrants might have entered the U.S.
legally with the intention of either applying for exit visas
if and when they needed them, or not returning to Mexico
at all.[4]

Mexican immigrants from nearly every state in the U.S. returned to Mexico in ever-increasing numbers as the Great Depression deepened. The majority of the 21,706 who crossed the border between July 1 and December 31, 1930, listed Texas as their last place of residence, but 40.7 percent named midwestern and even eastern states: Illinois, Michigan, Indiana, Iowa, Kansas, Missouri, Nebraska, Ohio, Pennsylvania, the Dakotas, and Wisconsin. By January 1931, the percentage of repatriates listing Texas and other southern states as their last place of residence increased sharply, with a corresponding drop in the percentage of those from northern states. Boyce believed this was a seasonal phenomenon. Those who wished to leave the north did so in the early months of winter in order to escape the hardships of the cold weather in that region.[5]

Most repatriates arrived in dire straits. Invoking a familiar ethnic construction of transiency, the American consul at Matamoros, Tamaulipas, reported that repatriates "resemble gypsies as they usually return by either wagon or broken down motor car in which children, household furniture, and domestic animals are loaded." He estimated that fifteen hundred had left through the port of Brownsville, Texas, in the months of July, August, and September, 1931, half in family groups and an equal number of "floating labor"—that is, men and women without family or baggage. Although most listed an urban area as their last place of residence, Boyce believed that twenty-five percent were field workers who lived only part of the year in a city, while another twenty-five percent were urban dwellers year-round.[6]

Residents of border towns and cities in the northern part of Mexico found it difficult to accommodate the large number of repatriates who either attempted to settle in these areas or who found employment there and remained for a brief period in order to earn enough money to continue their journey. The local charity society of Saltillo, Coahuila, for example, provided meals for repatriates. There was, according to the American consul in that city, a "very noticeable desire on the part of the municipal authorities . . . to hasten their departure." He mentioned that repatriates in Monterrey, sixty miles northeast of Saltillo, were complaining of the uncharitable treatment they were receiving.[7] An organization run by prominent women in Monterrey did what it could to help repatriates, but lack of funds limited the extent of aid it could give.[8]

One group of repatriates who arrived in Monterrey in early November 1931 included twenty-eight men, women, and children in five trucks. They had traveled over the Laredo National Highway from Waco, Texas, with their furniture, clothing, agricultural implements, and "everything else they could carry with them." They camped on a vacant lot in front of Union Station in Monterrey and were surrounded by curious passersby who questioned them about their journey, where they were from, and what hardships they had endured. All were farmers who had lived in Waco for many years, according to a spokesperson for the group, and who were returning because of the depression. They remained in Monterrey long enough to rest and then continued on to Victoria, Tamaulipas, where they hoped to take up farming.[9]

The number of repatriates entering Monterrey increased as the month wore on. *El Porvenir*, the local newspaper, reported that one thousand men, women, and children, many completely destitute and dressed in rags, had arrived the day before. Funds donated by the governor, the chamber of commerce, and private individuals to provide these people with food and railroad tickets were exhausted, and a local charitable organization had asked the Mexican government to supply repatriates with free passage to their final destination, as another thousand repatriates were on their way from Laredo and were expected at any time. The government responded immediately by telephone and authorized the railway to issue free tickets.[10]

Upon arriving in Mexico during the depression, repatriates often found that economic conditions were as bad as or worse than those they had experienced in the United States. A number attempted to return to the U.S., only to discover that U.S. authorities were now enforcing immigration laws much more strictly than they had in the 1920s. In addition, many repatriates who allowed relief agencies to pay for their return journey to Mexico discovered that immigration officials refused to readmit them to the United States by citing the 1917 Immigration Law, which prohibited the entrance of any individual likely to become a public charge.[11]

The United States vice-consul in Mexico City reported to the secretary of state that fifteen thousand repatriates a month had entered Mexico from August through December 1931. "Despite this tremendous influx, the repatriates have apparently been satisfactorily reabsorbed into the nation with a minimum of friction," he wrote.[12] In order to help finance the expense of transporting and feeding repatriates, the Mexican government enacted a law requiring the registration of all foreigners residing in Mexico and the payment of a fee of 10 pesos or $3.50 (U.S.). The Mexican government's strategy of transporting repatriates in their or their families' home villages and towns facilitated the absorption of repatriates.

The hundreds of thousands of repatriates entering Mexico during the depression greatly strained government resources. Many were able to find relatives to help them find employment and housing, but others found that they had no friends or families to turn to. The Mexican government established several agricultural colonies specifically for repatriates, in the hope that returning Mexicans and Mexican Americans could become self-supporting within a brief period of time.

There were three types of government-run agricultural colonies in which repatriates could participate. First, the National Irrigation Commission (NIC) established agricultural colonies on irrigation projects and made land available to certain categories of agricultural workers, including repatriates, for the price of 270 to 300 pesos (89 to 100 dollars) to be paid in twenty-five annual installments, at four percent interest. Second, the federal government established a number of small colonies independent of irrigation projects throughout Mexico, some of which supported only a few families. Finally, state governments also set aside land for repatriates to establish agricultural colonies.[13]

In order to establish agricultural colonies for the hundreds of thousands of repatriates entering Mexico, Mexican citizens organized a campaign in 1932 to raise one-half million pesos. By mid-1933, their organization, the Comité Nacional de Repatriación had collected 250,000 pesos and had established two colonies, one at Pinotepa, Oaxaca, and the other at El Coloso, Guerrero. The land in the two locations was fertile and the water plentiful. A small group of repatriates from Detroit comprised the first colonists in the program. They settled at Hacienda El Coloso, near Acapulco, in December 1933 forming a small, experimental colony.[14]

A larger number of repatriates settled at Pinotepa, Oaxaca. By the end of 1933, eight hundred repatriates lived there. The Comité Nacional de Repatriación spent a large part of its budget in setting up the colony at Pinotepa and had little left for establishing other colonies. But the committee's goal was to establish a self-sufficient community at Pinotepa that would require little or no additional outside aid. The project proved to be expensive and short-lived.

The committee sold land to each family at Pinotepa on a long-term repayment basis and gave them tools, farm machinery, soap, and, each week, three cartons of cigarettes and one peso. The committee also provided families with food at the beginning of their stay. It purchased forty thousand pesos' worth of farm machinery for the colony, including tractors, and spent an additional fifteen thousand pesos for mules. In addition, colony organizers installed water pumps for irrigation and shower baths for workers. The head of the committee justified the expense of installing showers by reporting that repatriates had developed different habits while in the U.S. and preferred showers to baths: "these [shower] baths are in use all the time. That is one thing the repatriates learned in the United States."[15] Finally, the committee constructed an open-air theater for workers, designed for concerts, dances, and public fiestas.

Committee members expected the Pinotepa colony to accommodate a half million people, but their plans contained one major flaw: the choice of locale for the colony. One repatriate reported, "the insects, disease, and poisonous snakes are very bad there." A number of colonists died in the colony, he said, "sometimes one a day, sometimes two or three." The repatriate agreed with the committee's evaluation of the fertility of the land: "The soil is rich, all right. Lots of things grow there, mangos, pineapples, bananas, corn, watermelons, and various vegetables. But people who aren't born there can't live there very long." He had left the colony, he said, "because there was too much sickness." "We went there in March," he told a sociology student from the United States in 1933, "with seven hundred people and left in the middle of April. I don't think anyone is left there now."[16] The repatriate had not been to El Coloso colony in Guerrero, but he had heard that the climate and insect life were similar to those of Pinotepa. Mexican newspapers confirmed the colonists' complaints about the Pinotepa and El Coloso colonies.[17]

In addition to agricultural colonies set up by the Comité Nacional de Repatriación, the Mexican government also attempted to establish agricultural colonies for repatriates. Federal irrigation projects built during the administration of President Ortiz Rubio provided land and employment for some repatriates. These were located at Don Martín and San Carlos, Coahuila; Pabellón, Aguascalientes; Tula, Hidalgo; El Mante, Tamaulipas; Delicias, Chihuahua; and El Nogal, Coahuila. The largest of these was the Don Martín project, located in Coahuila, eighty miles west of Laredo, Texas. The Mexican government paid for the passage of fifteen hundred unemployed repatriates to the project from Mexico City.[18]

Some repatriates reported that they could make a good living by farming irrigated land on the Don Martín project. One noted, "I made 400 pesos clear, and this was my first year." Another repatriate, from Texas, made a profit of 500 pesos, and a repatriate from Colorado reported that he made "a living all right on my crops."[19] In 1933, the Don Martín irrigation project made thirty thousand hectares (seventy-five thousand acres) available for cultivation. Colonists had the option of buying land at 50 to 300 pesos per hectare (2.5 acres), or rent-

ing it on a share basis, paying twenty percent of the crop annually for rent. Some colonists had farms of one hundred hectares, but the majority were in the range of five to twenty-five
hectares.[20]

The Don Martín colony, however, did not live up to the
expectations of government leaders, who had hoped the project would help to make repatriates economically self-sufficient. Inadequate government funding and drought limited
its success. As early as 1931, the press reported that the Mexican government was making arrangements to transport unemployed workers from the Don Martín project.[21] To remedy
the situation, President Lázaro Cárdenas distributed about
three thousand hectares to residents at Don Martín in 1936.
He then transferred several thousand unemployed workers,
the majority of whom were repatriates, from Don Martín project to two other irrigation projects in Tamaulipas. The Don
Martín project also suffered from a prolonged drought between 1937 and 1939, which brought about the demise of this
agricultural colony. By the end of 1939, thirty-six thousand
colonists were receiving aid from the Mexican government because of the depressed conditions at the Don Martín project.[22]

Other irrigation projects were only slightly more successful
in establishing agricultural colonies. Although irrigation projects offered repatriates who had some resources an opportunity to acquire fertile land at low prices, few benefitted since
most repatriates were destitute.[23] Repatriates without means to
purchase land remained unemployed, worked for others, or
petitioned for ejido land.

Ejidos (land the Mexican government allotted to communities for parcelling out to individual members to farm) provided a few repatriates with land, although here also,
repatriates found disappointment and extreme hardship. For
example, in one ejido village, Etucuaro, Michoacán, the eleven
hundred villagers viewed repatriates as outsiders who were
more American than Mexican. Although every adult male in
the community had been to the U.S. to work at least once,
most had not been there during the previous five years, and

villagers distinguished between migrants who returned home each year and repatriates who had settled for long periods of time in the United States.[24]

The community owned the land that individual community members farmed. By the time repatriates arrived at Etucuaro in 1933, all the land in that particular ejido had been parceled out to 108 members of the community. The repatriates, along with others, petitioned the government for another grant of land. During the six months that it took for the petition to be approved, repatriates were without land and worked for others in the community to support themselves.[25]

Most repatriates were ill-equipped to farm. Some repatriates in Etucuaro had trucks they had brought from the United States. For example, one family, who had lived in the United States for twenty-three years, brought a truck filled with clothes, a sewing machine, a meat grinder, and a record player with a collection of records. None, however, brought farm machinery since the journey to Etucuaro was so long and the price of gasoline to run machinery was prohibitive.[26]

Repatriates who settled in other government-run projects did not fare any better, although both the federal government and state governments strained their resources to provide for repatriates during the depression. The state government of Chihuahua, for example, provided several hundred repatriate farmers with land near Villa Ahumada, property that had been confiscated from hacendados as a result of the Mexican Revolution. In addition, the Veracruz state government gave preference to repatriates for the establishment of agricultural colonies.[27] State governments also set up colonies in Durango, Sonora, Guanajuato, Sinaloa, Baja California, and Jalisco, and offered land at low prices to repatriates. Like the federal projects, these state initiatives faced the problems of insufficient land and inadequate funding to establish repatriates as self-sufficient farmers. As a consequence of these deficiencies, the economic prospects of repatriates in Mexico were not much better than they had been in the U.S.

Repatriated men were often unprepared for their new lives.

According to one study of 114 repatriates, over half entered occupations different from those they had held in the United States. Of the repatriados who had the least difficulty in adjusting, most arrived with money, tools, or equipment, which allowed them to buy property or establish small businesses. One repatriated man who owned a grocery store brought four hundred pesos from the United States. Another came with shoe-repair equipment that he had purchased in Los Angeles for $1,300 and opened a shoe repair shop in Mexico.[28] But relatively few of these men had money to invest, since they had left the United States under desperate circumstances.

Women, too, had a difficult time adjusting to life in Mexico. Women earned extremely low wages compared to men, often only twenty-five percent of men's wages, which averaged between fifty centavos and one peso a day for laborers. James Gilbert interviewed one repatriated woman who supported herself and four children by working in a restaurant for only four pesos a month plus meals for her family. Another woman he interviewed in Zamora earned only three pesos a month, plus meals, working at a lunch stand in the marketplace.[29]

Those women who did not work outside their homes, particularly rural women, found that in Mexico they had less freedom to be in public places; such women complained that they were expected to spend nearly all of their time at home working.[30] In addition, customary practices in Mexico concerning dress and demeanor often seemed foreign and restrictive to repatriadas. One woman newly arrived from the United States did not like the way women dressed in the Mexican village to which she had moved: "Here the girls all dress alike, in black. But I'll never dress in black in all my life. Here it seems that when a girl is married, it's all over."[31]

Both women and men experienced hostility and violence from Mexicans who perceived them as foreigners. One repatriado from California explained: "On the ranch they asked me, 'where you come from?' And then I say, 'United States of America.' They say, 'You ——! What you doing here for, to eat the little bread we have. Why you no stay there.' Then I say, 'this is my country. I was born here. I come to see my brother, not because I had to leave.' But they say, 'you been over there long time. You stay there.'"[32] Similarly, a woman in Monterrey complained about her co-workers in the factory where she was employed: "Over at the factory, they call us Tejanas although actually we have only passed through Texas . . . I didn't speak Spanish very well when I first came here."[33]

Children, especially older ones, often found the transition to life in Mexico painful as well. They were forced to leave friends behind. Many had been born in the United States and were leaving their homeland to go to a foreign country to live.[34] One eleven-year-old girl told an interviewer that she wanted to return to the United States because she could not speak Spanish: "I would be in the fifth grade there, but here, no, because I didn't know how to read and write Spanish."[35] Another child, a Mexican American from Los Angeles, described police harrassment he and his friends experienced in Aguascalientes: "Well, they call us Northerners and we attract attention because we always talk English among ourselves. One time a cop heard us talking English and he called us over and bawled us out. He asked us what nationality we were and we said 'Mexicans.' 'Well,' he said, 'why don't you talk Spanish? When you are in Mexico, talk Spanish!' He said he would put us in the can if he heard us talking English." Such experiences must have been perplexing as well as painful to children who had left the U.S. because they were perceived to be Mexican and not American.[36]

Repatriates, young and old, were often rejected by Mexicans. A woman in Mexico City expressed her dislike for repatriates: "Most of us here in Mexico do not look on these repatriates very favorably. It doesn't please us much that these people who were discontented and thinking only of their own personal interests should come back here after running away when there was troublesome times here, and expect us to greet them with celebrations of fireworks and brass bands."[37] Employers often discriminated against repatriates in hiring. One ranch owner stated, "We prefer our own men; we pay too little for repatriados. They are used to $3, $4, or $5 a day and don't like to work for so little, so they are lazy."[38] Another employer, an American, reported that he was reluctant to hire repatriates because, as he put it, they "get too smart and spoil" the other workers.[39]

Repatriates had expected to find a refuge in Mexico from prejudice and discrimination. They had hoped that life would be easier among those they assumed to be their own people. Instead, they discovered that Mexicans often viewed them as Americans. In the United States, they had found that they could never become Americans, and now, in what was supposed to be their home country, they were not Mexicans. James Gilbert, a student from the University of Southern California, interviewed repatriates in several villages in 1933 and 1934. Gilbert found that the majority of his interviewees wished to return to the United States, either immediately or as soon as economic conditions there improved.[40]

Repatriates found, however, that the United States Immigration Bureau had limited the issuance of nonimmigrant visas and that it was increasingly difficult to cross the border surreptitiously. Also, U.S. immigration officials refused admission to nearly all Mexicans who had voluntarily participated in repatriation programs. Repatriates learned to their dismay that county officials had lied to them by assuring Mexican immigrants and Mexican Americans that they could return to the U.S. whenever they wanted. Officials had persuaded Mexicans to leave voluntarily rather than risk formal deportation, which would make returning to the U.S. a felony, but these same officials had stamped "Los Angeles Department of Charities" on the back of repatriates' visas. In doing so, they alerted immigration authorities to the fact that these repatriates had received county relief and, therefore, could be excluded from entrance into the U.S. on the grounds that they were "likely to become a public charge."[41] As a result, immigration from Mexico to the United States remained at a trickle throughout the 1930s. In the end, for Mexicans caught in a legal and cultural limbo between the U.S. and Mexico, repatriation became a kind of exile to nowhere.

6

CLASS WAR IN THE FIELDS:
Workers, Growers, and New Deal Reformers

Repatriation began to slow after 1932. During the four-year period from the beginning of 1929 to the end of 1932, more than 365,000 Mexican immigrants and Mexican Americans left the United States for Mexico. The number of repatriates became smaller each subsequent year, though more than 90,000 left in the years 1933–1937 and little return migration took place during the decade. As a consequence, the Mexican population in California and the rest of the U.S. dropped for the first time in eighty years.[1] In 1930, before formal repatriation began, there were approximately 650,000 Mexican immigrants in the United States, over one-third of whom lived in California.[2] Ten years later, the Mexican-born population of the United States had decreased by almost half.[3]

Repatriation programs succeeded in reducing the number of Mexicans on relief rolls, although numbers were never large to begin with. The programs did not, of course, end the Great Depression, but they did deflect attention from failed government economic policies. While repatriation had little effect on the course of the depression, it changed the ethnic makeup of California's farm labor force. The removal of Mexicans coincided with a massive in-migration of tenant farmers, sharecroppers, and destitute unemployed workers from drought-stricken areas in the United States, and, by 1936, Anglo workers comprised up to two-thirds of farm labor.[4]

The "whitening" of the farm labor force altered perceptions of farm workers in California and resulted in the inauguration of state and federal programs to study the needs of farm workers in the state and also the formation of a national labor union of agricultural workers. Government authorities found poor living conditions less tolerable when endured by white "American" workers than by those perceived to be foreign and temporary, and as a result of the new programs, conditions for some (mainly white) agricultural workers dramatically improved.

The federal government established New Deal programs to address the problems of farm workers in all regions of the country, including the Southwest. The California state government also addressed such problems. For example, the Division of Rural Rehabilitation, established by the California State Emergency Relief Administration in 1934, held three housing conferences in 1934 and 1935. As a result of the conferences, the federal Resettlement Administration proposed building twenty labor camps. By 1941, the Resettlement Administration had built eighteen migrant-labor camps in California.[5]

The Resettlement Administration built the first two camps at Arvin and Marysville. Each housed 175 to 450 families. These camps and those that followed were similar in construction. Houses or tents for workers were made of wood, metal, or canvas. They rested on raised platforms and surrounded the camp's community buildings. The community buildings included a delousing unit, an assembly room and nursery, a utility building, an isolation unit for those with contagious diseases, a first-aid room and children's clinic, a garbage area, a kitchen, a warehouse and pump house, and sixty shower-baths and toilets. In addition, the manager of the camp had an office and private quarters. The camp also had a recreation field. Workers paid rent of ten cents per day or two hours of labor per week at the camp. A sense of community developed in the camps, as camp residents established their own newsletters and organized social meetings, ball clubs, and child-care committees.

Mexican migrant families benefited from the improvement of living conditions for Anglo migrant workers as well, since many primarily Anglo camps also housed Mexican farm workers. In the end, however, the improvements were inadequate, as government programs to build housing for farm workers were insufficient to accommodate the quarter-of-a-million workers in California's fields at the height of the harvest season. The eighteen camps, housing 175 to 450 families, served primarily as models of what could be, while the majority of migrant workers continued to live in shanty towns, along irrigation ditches, and in auto camps.

The federal government not only conducted investigations of living conditions of farm workers but also of labor relations on California farms. These investigations focused on a number of employer practices, including manipulation of repatriation programs. California farm employers initially opposed repatriation, but they later used the programs to break agricultural strikes. This reversal revealed both the constraints under which agricultural employers operated in trying to maintain a labor force perceived as foreign, and the strategies they developed to get around or to manipulate these constraints to their advantage. Similarly, the Los Angeles Chamber of Commerce discouraged repatriation until Mexican immigrants organized and made demands for higher wages; only then did officials promote repatriation. At the same time, officials were careful not to jeopardize the region's labor supply permanently. "We need the Mexican in agriculture," George P. Clements, director of the agriculture department of the Los Angeles Chamber of Commerce, exclaimed, speaking for most California growers. He urged, "instead of harassing

Mexicans in an effort to scare them out of the country, efforts should be made to maintain as much of the local Mexican population as possible."[6]

Other agricultural employers in the Southwest, as well, initially saw repatriation as a threat to their control over the workplace and campaigned to end the drive. On May 12, 1931, the Chamber of Commerce of Douglas, Arizona, met to discuss the possibility of repatriating Mexicans who were on their relief rolls. Douglas charitable organizations were giving assistance to two hundred families, or approximately one thousand people, ninety percent of whom were Mexican. These were legal immigrants, many of whom had American-born children, according to a member of the board of directors of the Chamber of Commerce. Members of the board had learned of Los Angeles County's repatriation program and were interested in lightening their relief load by following the Los Angeles example and by returning as many Mexican immigrants as they could persuade to leave.[7]

By the next month, however, the board of directors had changed its mind. The *Douglas Daily Dispatch* reported that local fruit and truck farmers feared a labor shortage, such as that reported by Southern California farmers, if Mexican immigrants were repatriated from the area. "It might not be so grave a situation were it not for the fact that it is far less easy for the Mexicans to get back into the United States to seek employment than it was a few years ago," the writer pointed out. The article concluded by stating a truism of industrial agriculture that California farmers had been expressing for some time: "An ample labor population is one of the essentials to progress in normal times."[8]

Indeed, in early 1931, Arthur G. Arnoll, secretary and general manager of the Los Angeles Chamber of Commerce, had cautioned Charles P. Visel, director of the Los Angeles Citizens' Committee on Coordination of Unemployment Relief, about "upsetting the whole Mexican population by wholesale raids."[9] He described the deportation and repatriation program as a "conspiracy against agricultural labor, particularly the Mexican." According to Arnoll, the expulsion of Mexicans from the county had stirred up nativist sentiments. "The slogan has gone out over the city and is being adhered to—'employ no Mexican while a white man is unemployed; get the Mexican back into Mexico regardless by what means.' All this without taking into consideration the legality of the Mexican's status of being here," he wrote to Clements. "It is a question of pigment, not a question of citizenship or right," he continued. Arnoll's main concern was not with racial discrimination but with the effect repatriation would have on the agricultural labor supply. He feared that unless the Chamber of Commerce was able to stop deportation and repatriation of Mexicans, agricultural employers in the county would find themselves "high and dry as far as agricultural labor is concerned."[10]

Clements heeded Arnoll's warning and formed an immigration committee of Chamber of Commerce members to deal with the problem. The committee contacted the Mexican consul in Los Angeles, Rafael de la Colina, in late April 1931 about publicity in Mexican newspapers concerning the deportation and repatriation programs. The committee asked de la Colina to attend its next meeting to discuss the "weird tales of opposition" to Mexicans in Los Angeles that had been reported in the Mexican press, what basis they had in fact, and how to correct them if it were determined they were false.[11] The Mexican consul attended the meeting and promised to do all he could to correct the stories that were circulating in Mexico about mistreatment of Mexican immigrants in Los Angeles, according to Eugene Overton, a Chamber of Commerce official.[12]

The Chamber of Commerce subsequently contacted newspapers, radio stations, business establishments, and Mexican commercial agents in an effort to dispel rumors that might encourage repatriation. In May, the chamber wrote to the Los Angeles *Evening Express* and *La Opinión*, the Spanish-language newspaper in Los Angeles, asking that neither paper print unfounded rumors that might "unduly offend the sensibilities of a foreign nation."[13] The same month, Lewis Weiss, Manager of the KMPC Radio Station, agreed to have a statement read on-the-air aimed at calming the Mexican immigrant community in Los Angeles.[14]

Throughout the rest of 1931 and 1932, the Chamber of Commerce continued its efforts to end, or at least limit, the repatriation of Mexicans from Los Angeles County. In addition, the Chamber worked to organize unemployment relief for Mexican workers and to establish a labor bureau to solve the problem of access to Mexican labor in times of perceived shortages.

In 1933, however, the Chamber reversed its position opposing repatriation. That year, farm workers waged the largest number of strikes in the history of California agriculture, with Mexican workers active in every one. Farm wages hit their lowest point in 1933, at the same time that prices for California crops began rising and the demand for fruits and vegetables increased, so that total shipments were up from the previous year.[15] The U.S. Department of Agriculture reported that "the sharp advance in the prices of nearly all farm products since February 1933 is likely to increase farmers' gross income for production in 1933 over the unusually low income of 1932."[16] The report proved accurate. Although California farmers received higher prices for their crops in 1933 and their gross income increased from the previous year, however, they did not raise workers' wages. Farm workers protested by striking against their employers all around the state. The immediate response by growers was to call for the expulsion of Mexicans from the country.

The first strike took place in El Monte in Los Angeles County. Mexican workers, most of whom lived in an El Monte Valley barrio called Hick's Camp, struck for higher wages from Japanese berry growers in June 1933.[17] Berry pickers were hired in family groups, and their wages had averaged between fifteen and twenty cents an hour per person. They asked growers to raise their wages to twenty-five cents per hour and, when growers refused, they threatened to strike. The Confederación de Uniones Obreros Mexicanos (CUOM) organized the strike and had the cooperation and support of the Cannery and Agricultural Workers Industrial Union (C&AWIU). Berry pickers, with C&AWIU support, succeeded in expanding the strike until some seven thousand workers in berry, onion, and celery crops were participating throughout Los Angeles County.[18]

The strike came at the height of the berry-picking season. Growers immediately brought in strike breakers. Filipinos, Anglos, and Mexicans, as well as Los Angeles school children, replaced strikers as the job action wore on. By the time growers agreed to most of the strikers' terms in early July, the berry season was almost over. According to the terms of the agreement reached by the Mexican union, now named the Confederación de Uniones de Campesinos y Obreros Mexicanos (CUCOM), and the Japanese growers, employers were to pay berry pickers a minimum wage of $1.50 for nine hours work or 20 cents per hour for those not hired on a daily basis. They were also to recognize CUCOM as the bargaining agent for its members, give preference to union members when hiring, and discharge strikebreakers.[19] Japanese growers refused to discharge the native Anglo workers who had replaced strikers, but they agreed to replace Japanese aliens, Filipinos, and Mexicans, in that order, with workers who had been on strike.[20]

As the days passed, however, it seemed more and more evident to workers that the growers would not live up to their promise. More than five hundred families, or approximately twenty-seven hundred workers, had not been rehired, and on July 12 many of the unemployed Mexicans in El Monte demonstrated against berry growers. The demonstrators complained that they were without food or resources, since their strike fund was exhausted.[21] The Mexican workers threatened violence within twenty-four hours if they were not rehired, and their union, CUCOM, brought suit against the Japanese growers for breach of contract. The suit stated that "no part of those men affected by [the] strike had been returned to work and that about 2,000 men who were employed as strike breakers are still doing the work," and asked for one hundred thousand dollars in damages.[22] The union's attorney cautioned members involved in the strike not to accept employment until the case had been resolved.[23]

Members of the Los Angeles Chamber of Commerce were alarmed at these developments. They feared that labor agitation could spread and that publicity about militant Mexican workers could lead to increased nativism and agitation for immigration restriction, which might permanently cut off their supply of cheap Mexican immigrant labor. George Clements wrote to Francisco Palomares, secretary of the San Joaquin Valley Agricultural Labor Bureau, requesting that he travel to El Monte and convince unemployed workers to go to Mexico. In addition, Clements ordered a survey of Hick's Camp to determine how many of its Mexican residents were citizens.[24]

Clements learned that over half of the residents were first- or second-generation U.S. citizens. He proposed that employment be found for this group and repatriation offered to the rest. Repatriation would have to be voluntary, he concluded, and he suggested advising Mexican immigrants of the possibility of acquiring land through one of the Mexican government's colonization projects.[25] Arthur Arnoll, another member of the Chamber of Commerce, concluded that the situation warranted drastic action and that it was imperative to "get some of these people going back, American citizens or otherwise."[26]

Demonstrating the powerful influence of agricultural interests in California, Clements arranged a meeting with the Japanese and Mexican consuls, the county sheriff, and representatives of the county welfare office, the state Division of Labor Statistics, and the federal immigration office to find a solution to the danger posed by unemployed and militant Mexican workers in the El Monte district. Clements proposed that work in other areas of the state be found for unemployed workers from Hick's Camp and that the Department of Charities provide unemployed workers with relief. He urged the sheriff's office to agree to keep the peace and prevent violence from erupting. He also appealed to the Japanese and U.S. authorities to treat the strike as a domestic affair, not as an international one involving the Japanese and Mexican governments.[27]

The Japanese consul reported to Clements that all two thousand families who picked berries for Japanese growers would soon be without work, as the season was nearly over. The consul estimated that only one thousand families would be needed by mid-July and five hundred fewer the following week.[28] Clements contacted Frank Palomares about the possibility of sending these workers to the San Joaquin Valley to work in the cotton fields there.[29] At a July 17 meeting called by Clements, Palomares agreed to find work for the unemployed workers. He and F. A. Steward, secretary of the California–Arizona Cotton Association, arranged to find work for five hundred families immediately, five hundred more the following week, and another five hundred on the first of August.[30] Palomares, Clements, the county sheriff, and a representative of the Los Angeles County Welfare Department agreed to assign an undercover agent from the sheriff's office to try to convince Mexican immigrants in Hick's Camp to leave the country and accept the Mexican government's offer of free land in agricultural colonies in Baja California and Nayarit.[31]

On July 19, W. N. Cunningham, of the United States Department of Labor's Employment Service in Santa Ana, submitted a report to J. H. Fallin of the Farm Labor Division of the Employment Service in Los Angeles, warning that Mexican union members in Hick's Camp who were going to be sent to the San Joaquin Valley to work in the cotton fields were likely to agitate for strikes there. He quoted one worker as saying, "If there is no strike in the San Joaquin Valley now there will be one when we get there." He concluded by reporting that there were enough unemployed workers in Orange and Los Angeles counties to fill the labor needs in the valley and suggested using these workers rather than taking a chance on those from Hick's Camp.[32] Fallin informed Palomares of the report, and Palomares immediately withdrew his offer to use unemployed berry pickers.

Joining in the fight against striking workers, the Los

Angeles Department of Charities, at a meeting held on July 21, agreed to withdraw relief funds from families refusing to accept employment in the San Joaquin Valley. However, since Palomares had indicated that he would not take workers from El Monte, this did not affect them. The county agreed to continue to extend relief to the unemployed workers in Hick's Camp because, as Clements wrote to Arnoll, "unfortunately, under the Reconstruction Finance money, we are compelled to feed all who are hungry."[33]

Many were, indeed, in desperate straits. Working and living conditions for all farm workers deteriorated during the 1930s, but the depression was especially disastrous for Mexican workers.[34] Mexican families earned one-sixth of the national average of $1,784 in 1935. That year, the California State Relief Administration reported that a family required a minimum of $780 to pay for food, utilities, and rent. The Heller Committee for Research in Social Economics at the University of California established $972 for what it termed a "health and decency" budget for an average family in 1935. Yet, a study of 775 Mexican families in California conducted that year revealed an average annual income of only $289.[35]

High unemployment among Mexican Americans and Mexican immigrants accounted for their low earnings, as Enrique A. Gonzales, a Mexican consular inspector, discovered when he visited the Southwest in 1932 to determine the impact of the depression on Mexican workers in the United States. He found that as many as half of all Mexican workers in the region had no jobs.[36] One contemporary writer noted that Anglo workers threatened violence to employers "who hired Mexicans rather than unemployed Americans."[37] Competition for farm jobs became especially severe as unemployed city workers moved to the countryside in search of farm jobs. More than 1,540,000 left cities for farms in 1932, while 468,000 migrated from farms to cities. As a result, the 1933 farm population of 32 million was the largest in U.S. history, as two workers competed for each farm job, on average, during that year.[38]

At the same time, wages for agricultural workers in California fell dramatically between 1930 and 1933. Farm workers who had been earning a monthly salary of $60.75 in 1930 earned only $30.12 in 1933. Daily wages dropped from an average of $2.55 in 1930 to $1.40 in 1933, so that some workers were earning only 15 to 16 cents an hour.[39]

It is hardly surprising, then, that Mexican farm workers demanded higher wages. Many had lived and worked in the U.S. for years and, they believed, had proved themselves deserving of a living wage. They held on to their homes and what was left of their communities, maintaining that they were entitled to remain in what had become their country. Many also took an active role in organizing strikes and unions between 1933 and 1939 to protect their economic position.

Growers reacted to the growing militancy of farm workers by resorting to violence and terrorism. Increasingly, they relied on the precedent set by government-sanctioned repatriation programs in 1931–33 in using intimidation and expulsion to rid the country of Mexican immigrants and Mexican American "foreigners." During a 1933 cotton strike in the San Joaquin Valley, for example, growers held mass parades, in which they marched with sawed-off shotguns. When they arrived at the strike area, they shot tear gas at striking workers. Local sheriffs sided with the growers, deputizing them and arresting workers whom they identified as strike leaders. One sheriff told an interviewer: "We protect our farmers here in Kern County. They are our best people. They are always with us. They keep the county going. They put us in here and they can put us out again, so we serve them. But the Mexicans are trash. They have no standard of living. We herd them like pigs."[40]

Between ten thousand and twelve thousand workers, over half of whom were Mexican Americans and Mexican immigrants, participated in the cotton strike that took place in Kern, Kings, and Tulare counties in the San Joaquin Valley. Organized by the C&AWIU, the strike lasted for three weeks during the fall of 1933. Growers recruited children as strikebreakers and arranged to import thousands of cotton pickers from Texas, as well.[41] In Pixley, a small farm community fifteen miles south of Tulare, growers attacked a group of strikers who were peacefully gathered to listen to strike leader Pat Chambers. One grower clubbed a striker to the ground and then shot him to death. Other growers shot at retreating strikers. Thirteen workers were shot, and two, Dolores Hernández and Delfino D'Ávila, died. Eight growers faced charges in the shootings, but all were acquitted.[42]

A similar confrontation took place in Arvin on the same day, resulting in the death of one Mexican striker, Pedro Subia, and the wounding of several others. Instead of arresting growers, authorities charged strikers with murder and rioting. Federal and state authorities intervened in the strike and imposed a compromise wage increase of seventy-five cents per hundred pounds of cotton picked, fifteen cents more than growers had offered strikers and twenty-five cents less than farm workers demanded. During the negotiations to end the strike, the California Emergency Relief Administration, which had been providing relief funds to strikers, withdrew assistance in an effort to force strikers to accept the seventy-five–cent offer. Farm workers ultimately succumbed to grower violence, intimidation, the withdrawal of relief, and the deportation of Mexican strike leaders, and they accepted the terms.[43]

The strike marked the end of C&AWIU effectiveness as a union and the beginning of an unrelenting drive by California growers to break strikes and union organizations. Following the strike, growers met with the Agricultural Labor Subcommittee of the state Chamber of Commerce in Los Angeles in early November 1933 and proposed that a citizens' committee be formed to address the threat of strikes and unionization on California farms. The citizens' committee met and formed the Associated Farmers of California, a grower organization dedicated to the use of force in suppressing farm worker militancy.[44]

In the Imperial Valley, growers resorted to what one writer called "unrestrained physical violence and arbitrary arrest" when lettuce workers went on strike for higher wages in 1933.[45] City, county, and state police and American Legionnaires attacked workers with clubs and tear gas.[46] At Azteca Hall in Brawley, during a meeting of striking workers—the majority of whom were Mexican men, women, and children—the county sheriff barricaded all exits and fired tear gas into the meeting hall. Union members had to break windows to escape the fumes. Once strikers left, the deputies entered the hall and destroyed everything inside, including a duplicating machine, a stove, and a typewriter.[47]

Growers in the valley made it apparent they believed themselves to be above the law. At one point, authorities in the Imperial Valley detained representatives of the Los Angeles Regional Labor Board and the state labor commissioner, who had come to observe the strike. Two of the official observers reported that the captain of the state highway patrol told them: "You men should get out of here. You are hurting our work. We don't want conciliation. We know how to handle these people, and where we find trouble makers we'll drive them out, if we have to 'sap' them."[48] In the face of violence and intimidation, workers called off the strike on January 18, 1934.[49]

During another strike in 1934, in Contra Costa County, the Associated Farmers again used terror and vigilante action against Mexican workers. A group of seventy-five growers, all belonging to the Associated Farmers, escorted strikers to the county line and threatened their lives if they returned. The county sheriff then deputized the growers, who subsequently arrested strikers who were picketing farms in the county. Unable to counter state and grower power, workers called off the strike.[50]

The C&AWIU limped along until 1935, when state authorities arrested its leaders (on charges that they were proposing to overthrow the government), deported Mexican strike leaders, and imprisoned others. Other unions, like the American Federation of Labor (AFL), attempted to move into the breach. In 1935, the AFL tried to organize field workers and packing-house workers in one statewide union. AFL leaders were divided in their support of an agricultural union. Paul Scharrenberg, secretary of the California Federation of Labor, visited California and summed up the stance of the AFL national leadership: "only fanatics are willing to live in shacks or tents and get their heads broken in the interest of migratory laborers."[51]

It was not until native-born whites dominated the farm labor force that a successful union organizing drive of migrant workers took place again. In 1937, the United Cannery, Agricultural, Packing and Allied Workers of America (UCAPAWA) organized field and packing-shed workers in one union, a strategy that took advantage of the more financially secure position of packing-shed workers. Since packing-shed workers had nearly year-round work, they could provide a stable financial base for the union. However, UCAPAWA had limited success in strikes of field and packing-shed workers in 1938 and 1939. By 1941, it, too, had fallen victim to grower power and vigilante action by the Associated Farmers of California.

The tactics of the Associated Farmers did not go unnoticed in the rest of the country. New Deal reformers who had mediated during the 1933 cotton strike in California had witnessed growers' strategies. When Congress empowered a subcommittee of the Senate Committee on Education and Labor to investigate violations of the right of free speech and assembly and interference with the right of labor to organize and bargain collectively, farm labor in California became part of the subcommittee's investigations.[52]

The La Follette Civil Liberties Committee, as it came to be known, was chaired by Senator Robert M. La Follette, Jr., of Wisconsin. It conducted investigations between 1936 and 1940 throughout the country. These investigations uncovered a pattern of anti-union activities that violated workers' civil liberties. The committee documented employer use of machine guns and "sickening gas" (similar to tear gas) to break strikes, armed guards to intimidate workers both on and off

company property, strikebreakers, and company spies to infil-
trate worker organizations.[53]

Similar employer violations in California agriculture were
the subject of a limited inquiry by the La Follette Committee
late in 1938. This investigation focused on the efforts of the
Associated Farmers of California to break agricultural labor
strikes, and although it was cut short because funds ran out,
the evidence accumulated was enough to prompt Towne Ny-
lander, West Coast regional director of the National Labor
Relations Board (NLRB), to conclude that it would "be of a
great deal of help to us in the administering of the [National
Labor Relations] Act in this Region if the investigations become public."[54] Although agricultural workers had been ex-
pressly excluded from the National Labor Relations Act of
1935, it was becoming clear to committee members and the
NLRB that farm workers should be protected in their efforts
to organize and bargain collectively. A full inquiry followed in
1939 after the publication of two books that brought national
attention to the plight of agricultural workers in California:
John Steinbeck's novel, *The Grapes of Wrath*, which examined
the lives of white migratory workers in California, and Carey
McWilliams's critique of agricultural production and labor relations in California, *Factories in the Field*.[55] The La Follette
Committee called four hundred witnesses and gathered docu-
ments and testimony that clearly demonstrated the need for
protection of the rights of farm workers to organize.[56]

The La Follette Committee brought to public attention the
industrial nature of farming and farm labor in California. Significantly, it also placed the California experience in a national
context. University of California economist Paul S. Taylor,
testifying at the La Follette Committee hearings, described
California agricultural production as large-scale corporate
farming where specialized crops, large state-funded irrigation
projects, huge landholdings, and wage labor predominated.[57]
Taylor told the committee that, according to the 1935 Census
of Agriculture, four percent of farms dominated one-fourth
of all crop land in the state and less than seven percent of

farms in California held forty-two percent of all farm land. Furthermore, the majority of farm laborers in California worked on large farms. Farming was not a family affair, he told committee members, but big business.[58]

The La Follette Committee heard testimony from local officials, agricultural experts, growers, and workers on the difficulties farm workers faced in organizing unions and negotiating a living wage for themselves. In the process, the committee established that farm workers in California were not hired hands, moving up the agricultural ladder to become farm owners, but were proletarianized wage workers who desperately needed the protection of federal labor legislation afforded other industrial workers. Investigators found that employers' associations "played a leading role in fixing labor policies, and have been able to impose their influence upon the social and economic structure of the State." The committee denounced the Associated Farmers of California for "producing economic injustice, industrial unrest, class violence and the myriad evils that flow from industrial autocracy."[59]

The La Follette Committee's investigation clearly revealed the gap between the myth of the family farm and the reality of industrial agricultural production in California. As Paul S. Taylor pointed out to the committee, "the great strikes which periodically wrack the agricultural industry of California and may give rise to violations of civil liberties are not strikes between [an] 'American farmer' and his 'hired man.' In California, as in other parts of the country, the conspicuous instances of labor strife in agriculture occur between those individuals or corporations who are more properly called 'agricultural employers' [and wage workers]." Taylor went on to argue that California had experienced so many more agricultural strikes in the 1930s than any other area of the country because "here, the number of farm operators who really are 'agricultural employers' is so large, and because they, with their great number of employees, form an industrialized pattern."[60]

The most outspoken supporter of California farmers, George P. Clements, chairman of the Agricultural Department of the Los Angeles Chamber of Commerce, revealed that agricultural employers themselves no longer believed the myth. Clements wrote a memorandum to another member of the Chamber of Commerce saying: "we on the land have always recognized that California agricultural labor requirements made impossible to those people so employed the full effects of American citizenship and the possibility of ever partaking of our normal standards of life."[61]

Meanwhile, Taylor and others argued forcefully that the situation of agricultural workers in California—who had long suffered from low wages, inadequate living conditions, job insecurity, and low social status—was not the exception but, in fact, mirrored the plight of migrant workers all over the country. The violence, intimidation, and denial of workers' civil rights that the committee investigated in California, they argued, reflected agricultural labor relations in every region of the U.S. The committee learned that by 1933, thirty-three percent of all those employed in agriculture in the U.S. were wage laborers and sharecroppers. The Committee on Farm Tenancy, appointed by President Franklin D. Roosevelt in 1937, concluded that there was "an increasing tendency for the rungs of the [agricultural] ladder to become bars," preventing farm workers and sharecroppers from ever acquiring their own farms. Furthermore, they found, as the opportunities for farm workers to become farm owners dwindled, organization into unions became their only avenue of hope.[62]

The La Follette Committee also learned that while the power of agricultural unions had been exceptionally weak until 1933, farm workers had demonstrated their ability to join together in effective strikes after passage of the National Industrial Recovery Act (NIRA) of 1933. Farm workers throughout the country, they found, mistakenly believed that the act applied to them and thought that they had the protection of the federal government in protesting unfair farm labor practices and in demanding the right to organize and bargain collectively. Significantly, in 1930, U.S. farm workers organized only eight strikes, with eight thousand workers taking part. Even fewer workers went on strike in the next two years. However, in 1933 alone, nearly sixty thousand workers organized sixty-one strikes. Over half of these strikes, involving forty-eight thousand workers, took place in California. Henry Fowler, chief counsel of the La Follette Committee, described the strikes in California as some of the most violent in the nation in any occupation. By the time workers discovered they were not in fact covered by the NIRA, growers had mounted a full-scale attack on farm-worker unions and had resorted to strikebreaking tactics that went far beyond the La Follette Committee's definition of unfair labor practices.[63]

The committee found that civil and criminal disturbances had occurred in sixty-five strikes in thirty California counties between January 1, 1933, and July 1, 1939. Employers, led by the Associated Farmers of California, used firearms against workers in sixteen strikes, evicted and called for deportation of Mexican workers in fifteen strikes, and used a variety of forms of violence in an additional eight strikes. The committee concluded that grower action against strikers was well organized, and was therefore not a spontaneous reaction to workers' protests, as growers had claimed.[64]

The president of the Associated Farmers, Samuel P. Frisselle, told the committee that the organization was formed in response to the "subversive wave which had hit California, [and] due to the killings, as a result of killings at Pixley and the terrible situation which agriculture was facing, we went to our friends who were dependent upon the industry for help."[65] Frisselle identified the primary contributors to the organization as industrialists and those whose businesses depended upon the handling of agricultural products.[66] In order to break strikes, Frisselle told the committee, growers enlisted the help of local sheriffs who armed themselves with tear gas and machine guns. Responding to a cotton strike in Kern County, the under-sheriff bought a thousand dollars worth of sickening gas and swore in forty-five deputies. "As a result," the sheriff later reported in an interview, "there was fifty percent picketing all during the strike because we protected our farmers. The strikers didn't dare do nothing here. We had them covered and they knew it. They were afraid."[67]

Local law-enforcement officers played a decisive role in the course of workers' protests on California's farms, witnesses told the La Follette Committee. Sheriffs deputized employees of growers, many of whom were private guards, to disrupt strike activities. Chester P. Moore, managing secretary of the Western Growers' Protective Organization, testified before the La Follette Committee that during the Salinas lettuce strike of 1936, growers directed him "to take a group of ranch guards and have them deputized by the sheriff." Officials deputized between 100 and 150 guards during the course of the strike. Consequently, the Salinas strike, organized by the Mexican-dominated Fruit and Vegetable Workers Union, became a pitched battle as guards, state and local police, vigilantes, and imported thugs attacked four thousand or more lettuce packers and sympathizers. The NLRB reported that "the impression of these events obtained from the record is one of inexcusable police brutality, in many instances bordering on sadism."[68]

A number of witnesses testified to the committee that growers employed industrial spies to destroy unions in California. One witness, the sheriff of Contra Costa County, admitted to the La Follette Committee that he had directed an undercover agent to spy on meetings of the local Congress of Industrial Organizations (CIO) agricultural workers' union, UCAPAWA, and report back to the sheriff's office on planned union activities. The sheriffs of Sutter and Fresno counties both admitted that they had engaged in the same practice, and the sheriff of Fresno County reported that one of his agents was paid by the local Associated Farmers. Such agents made it possible for the Associated Farmers to compile a list of names of more than twenty thousand labor leaders and "liberals"— union sympathizers—which they then circulated among growers and law-enforcement agencies throughout the Southwest. The list was used to harass, deport, and discriminate against union members and supporters.[69] The committee also heard testimony that California growers routinely hired "scabs" (replacement workers) and thugs to break strikes. During the San Joaquin cotton strike of 1933, for example, growers made arrangements to recruit thousands of cotton pickers from Texas. They also were able to have local schools closed in a number of communities so that school children could replace striking farm workers in the fields.[70]

The committee gathered enough evidence to support a proposal for legislation to protect laborers' right of free speech and assembly and their right to organize and bargain collectively. On March 26, 1939, committee chairman La Follette introduced Senate Bill 1970 (S.1970) to "Eliminate Certain Oppressive Labor Practices Affecting Interstate and Foreign Commerce." The Oppressive Labor Practices Bill was the first piece of protective labor legislation proposed during the New Deal that did not specifically exclude agricultural workers from its provisions and, therefore, the first to give farm workers the same protection as other industrial workers in the country.

Although the bill failed, public notions of farm labor were redefined through the investigations of the La Follette committee and the press coverage it received. Growers and their supporters continued to call upon the myth of the family farm and the hired hand, but their arguments never again received the same unquestioning acceptance they had enjoyed before the La Follette Committee documented the industrial nature of agricultural production in California and made public its findings through hearings and congressional debates over the Oppressive Labor Practices Bill. The La Follette Committee's investigations also brought to public attention the danger certain "oppressive labor practices" posed to the civil liberties of all citizens.

The Oppressive Labor Practices Bill was, according to members of the House of Representatives who authored a companion bill, "by far the most important legislative proposal that this Congress could pass for the benefit of the working people of this country. Even more directly than the Wagner Act, this bill makes for industrial peace."[71] U.S. Attorney General Frank Murphy concurred, and he gave his support to the bill because he believed that it was crucial to the preservation of civil liberties, since one of its main objectives was "to prevent the invasion of civil rights by private interests." Murphy cited the 1938 investigations of the La Follette Committee into activities of the Associated Farmers in California as evidence that the civil rights of farm workers were in dire need of protection from the private interest of growers.[72]

The bill prohibited four categories of labor practices by employers that affected interstate and foreign commerce: the use of professional strikebreakers; the employment of armed guards to intimidate strikers; industrial espionage; and the use of what the La Follette Committee referred to as "industrial munitions"—machine guns, sawed-off shotguns, and sickening gas.[73] A subcommittee of the Committee on Education and Labor held hearings during May and June 1939 on S.1970 to review the La Follette Committee's investigations of violations of civil liberties within the four categories of oppressive labor practices.

Gerald D. Reilly, solicitor for the Department of Labor, pointed out that S.1970 complemented existing labor legislation and fit in with a four-fold program that the federal government had been promoting to set minimum working standards, to assert the government's power as a customer of industry (through government contracts) to raise such standards, to protect collective bargaining, and to provide services of mediation and arbitration in labor disputes. Reilly forcefully argued that the Oppressive Labor Practices Bill was "an appropriate and necessary part of the program designed to foster and promote economic democracy and industrial peace."[74]

Violations of the bill, as stated in section 6, would result in a fine of up to ten thousand dollars or six months of imprisonment, or both.[75] Section 203 penalized any person who held a loan from any United States agency who participated in oppressive labor practices. Should a borrower take part in one of the oppressive labor practices listed in the bill, the loan would become due and payable.[76] F. F. Hill of the Farm Credit Administration requested that this latter stipulation be amended to exclude farmers and their cooperative organizations, arguing that their inclusion would place a heavy administrative burden on the Farm Credit Administration and would make it more difficult for farmers to get loans.[77] Although approval of the amendment was a blow to labor, in striking contrast to earlier debates concerning federal labor legislation, this was the only request for exclusion of employers of agricultural labor from prohibition of oppressive labor practices. Other provisions penalizing farm employers remained in the bill.

On July 20, 1939, the subcommittee approved the bill, and on July 22, the Committee on Education and Labor also reported favorably. However, Senator Wallace H. White of Maine blocked its consideration in the next session of Congress. As a consequence, the bill did not reach the floor of the Senate until the following spring. In the meantime, the La Follette Committee continued to hold hearings in California and Washington, D.C. The committee listened to testimony in Los Angeles for twenty-eight days during December 1939 and January 1940, and in Washington, D.C., between May 2 and June 4, 1940, amassing evidence that workers in nearly every industry in the United States had been the targets of oppressive labor practices.[78]

By the time S.1970 came up for debate in the Senate, however, the war in Europe had escalated, and Congress and the president had shifted their focus and concern from domestic to international affairs. Many policy makers and legislators demanded that the government turn its attention away from the domestic reform and protection of labor to national preparedness and the defense of the nation.[79]

The interval between the first session of Seventy-Sixth Congress, when S.1970 was introduced, and the third session, when debate began, had provided time for opponents to build their assault on the bill. Senator Claude Pepper reported during the debate that he had been "deluged with telegrams from people" demanding that the La Follette bill be killed.[80] Senator Alexander Wiley of Wisconsin introduced an anticommunist slant to the debate when he spoke against the passage of the Oppressive Labor Practices Bill by urging his "fellow congressmen to recognize the urgency of undertaking a preparedness program in defense, in response to developments in Europe." The country, he argued, must be protected against the infiltration of a "fifth column." S.1970, he claimed, would "hamstring" defense measures by making it difficult for employers to question the political and economic philosophy of their workers and, as a consequence, communists would take over industries throughout the United States and instigate a revolution of the working class. He then read an excerpt from a letter written by Chester Wright, who claimed that a "Nazi fifth column" was organized "in Mexico," which, in his words, was "as large as our own whole Regular Army" and ready to invade the United States at any moment.[81]

Wiley continued his attack on the Oppressive Labor Practices Bill by arguing that passage of the bill would prevent citizens from possessing munitions for self-protection, and as a consequence, industry would be unable to protect its property from rioting foreigners. He suggested that the bill was part of a conspiracy by "a mob in which some foreign agent of a 'blitzkrieg' group is the moving force."[82] La Follette defended the bill, explaining that employers were not prohibited by the bill from questioning workers about their political alliances; S.1970 merely restrained employers from doing so without the knowledge of the worker being investigated. In the past, La Follette pointed out, many employers had hired detective agencies, such as the Pinkerton Detective Agency, to destroy unions and break strikes.[83]

Senator Walter F. George of Georgia attacked the bill on the grounds that it would apply to farmers, whose production, he argued, was far removed from commerce.[84] George warned that a provision giving the secretary of labor the power to investigate violations of the prohibition of oppressive labor practices would give the secretary "a power to crucify industry;

a power to destroy liberty of action; a power to destroy the industries of this country; and unless the productive capacity of American industries is kept up, there is no possible hope of preparation to meet any enemy, domestic or foreign."[85]

Senator Robert R. Reynolds of North Carolina proposed two amendments to S.1970 that reflected the preoccupation of many legislators with the need to defend industry from "an enemy within." These amendments provided that ninety percent of the work force of any manufacturer in the United States must be American (that is, citizens of the United States) and that the remaining ten percent alien workers must have applied for citizenship before being employed. In addition, the amendments prohibited members of the Communist Party and members of any "Nazi-bund organization" from employment on a work project prosecuted under S.1970. Both amendments passed on May 20 and May 27, 1940, respectively, and in the process transformed the Oppressive Labor Practices Bill from one protecting the rights of workers into a defense measure that could be used to deny them their civil rights, to break strikes, and to undermine union organizing—especially in California, where union leaders and union members were often members of the Communist Party and where Mexicans made up a large part of the work force.[86]

The Oppressive Labor Practices Bill passed in the Senate on May 27, 1940, by a vote of 47 to 20. An editorial in the *New York Times* scathingly criticized the bill. The Reynolds amendments, it stated, were probably unconstitutional, but "unconstitutional or not, the amendments carry in every syllable the mark of bigotry and injustice. It will be a black mark on the reputation of Congress if this provision, or anything like it, is allowed to become law."[87] It was not. The companion bill in the House of Representatives was set aside and allowed to die.[88]

The failure of the federal government to protect farm workers during the 1930s had tremendous consequences for the entrenchment of Mexican immigrants as a reserve labor force constructed as foreign and temporary. With the entrance of the U.S. into World War II, white native-born workers moved out of agricultural jobs and into war-related industries that paid higher wages, and Mexican immigrants once again dominated farm labor in California. California growers were able to convince the U.S. government to waive immigration restrictions and to use federal funds to recruit, allocate, and house Mexican workers. As a result, the U.S. and Mexico entered into a bilateral agreement, popularly known as the Bracero Program, to supply workers to agricultural employers, and large-scale Mexican immigration to the U.S. resumed. Renewed immigration from Mexico calmed the fears of growers who had worried that the preponderance of native-born white workers in the fields, who could not be repatriated or deported, jeopardized agricultural production during wartime because growers could not control wages.

Mexican immigrants and Mexican Americans soon dominated the farm labor force, and local, state, and federal interest in the health and welfare of farm workers dwindled. The Bracero Program limited participation to men, and agencies at first assumed only men would be working in the fields. Later, they ignored the presence of women, despite increasing awareness that both Mexican men and Mexican women were farm workers. Thus, the Bracero Program resuscitated and helped to perpetuate the perception of Mexicans as foreign, temporary, male workers, although renewed immigration from Mexico was anything but temporary. The Bracero Program lasted for twenty-two years, and many braceros settled permanently in the U.S. In addition, the recruitment of braceros stimulated a broader migration stream of Mexican workers, both women and men, into the U.S.

Representations of the work force as temporary and male influenced both government policies and growers' practices, which severely limited the economic participation of Mexican immigrants. Thus, the construction of Mexican immigrants and Mexican Americans as "birds of passage," not settlers, made it difficult for all Mexicans to establish the roots other immigrant groups had been able to establish, since public and private agencies could invoke this myth to justify ignoring the needs of Mexican Americans and Mexican immigrants and to justify expelling them from the country during economic depressions. The representation of Mexicans as male, temporary workers encouraged discrimination especially against Mexican women, who were relegated to the most exploitative jobs in the economy. In addition, government agencies were less likely to recognize the needs of Mexican immigrant and Mexican American women, since men supposedly dominated the temporary migrant stream. Thus, the ideology of the American Dream, including the myth of the family farm, was perpetuated on the backs of all Mexicans in the U.S., but in particular, on the backs of women.

The legislative process during the 1930s and 1940s was shaped by national ideologies and in turn shaped the legal status of Mexican American and Mexican immigrant men and women in the United States. The Oppressive Labor Practices Bill had been introduced at a time when industrialists and their supporters were mounting a well-organized assault on the power of labor unions. By 1943, however, an ideological reversal took place in the government's attitude toward labor. Moving away from New Deal sympathies toward labor, the federal government began regulating labor as a way of protecting business. Consequently there was little support for the adoption of national legislation that would have provided the now predominantly Mexican farm labor force with the protection necessary for successful and sustained union organization.[89]

Although the Oppressive Labor Practices Bill passed in the Senate in 1940, it never got beyond its introduction in the House of Representatives. Similarly, when Senator La Follette introduced S.2435, on April 3, 1942, to curtail the activities of employers' associations and citizens' committees such as the Associated Farmers of California, the bill expired in committee. Then, in 1943, for the first time since passage of the NLRA in 1935, both houses of Congress passed a bill contrary to the spirit of the NLRA. The Smith Act incorporated some of the antiradical provisions proposed in the Reynolds Amendments to S.1970. Culmination of the assault on labor-union strength came in 1947 with the passage of the Taft-Hartley

Act, which contained detailed regulation of labor relations with the express purpose of protecting employers from workers.[90]

Exclusion of farm workers from New Deal protective labor legislation and the failure of the Oppressive Labor Practices Bill (which would have included farm workers in such legislation), however, meant that farm workers were not covered by the restrictive Taft-Hartley Act. Later, in the 1960s, the United Farm Workers under César Chavez and Dolores Huerta turned exclusion to their advantage in calling for a secondary boycott, prohibited under the Taft-Hartley Act, to build a powerful agricultural union in California.[91] Chavez's and Huerta's ability to expose the weakness in this legislation worked initially to the union's advantage, but with the passage of the California Agricultural Labor Relations Act and the institutionalization of protective legislation, the strategy of using a secondary boycott was lost. Furthermore, growers were able to gain control of the Agricultural Labor Relations Board in California. The union's painful and often violent struggles for workers' rights, as well as California growers' attempts to position Mexican workers as temporary and foreign, emerged out of the legacy of workers' battles in the 1930s.

Mexican American and Mexican immigrant women and men who had stayed behind in the U.S. during the 1930s survived the depression with the knowledge that Mexicans were an unwanted people who could be expelled at any time. Repatriation and the publicity surrounding it not only reinforced existing ideas about Mexican immigrants and Mexican Americans as foreigners who were primarily young men working temporarily in the U.S., but actually gave credence to the idea that Mexicans indeed were not Americans—that repatriation was a consequence and a manifestation of their foreignness, and therefore proof of it. The construction of Mexican Americans and Mexican immigrants as alien made it possible for government agencies to continue to sponsor and support repatriation and to intimidate Mexicans in the U.S. without fear of sanctions.

Government involvement legitimized and established a precedent for the use of intimidation and expulsion to solve economic problems, a precedent that other agencies and groups could draw upon with relative impunity. Between 1939 and 1954, the federal government expelled three million Mexican immigrants and Mexican Americans from the country, using the military to carry out "Operation Wetback"—a name that both drew upon and naturalized the construction of Mexican Americans and Mexican immigrants as foreign, temporary, and illegitimate.

The conflict over who was entitled to economic opportunity in the United States and the strategies agricultural employers and Mexican farm workers used in this conflict revealed that the contestation was over not one, but two very different concepts of the American Dream. It was also an argument about how the imagined community of the American nation was to be peopled.[92] Growers, aided by state power, struggled to perpetuate an essentialized, normative image of who was American, based on racial and gender ideologies of white male individualism. Mexican farm workers, on the other hand, fought to reinscribe a promise of America that was dynamic and inclusive.

Thus, the American Dream was not one dream, but two dreams, each transformed through contestation for cultural, ethnic, and racial leadership among different immigrant and native-born groups. Rather than a story of exclusion from access to economic security—a story that includes a call for social justice through inclusion—the history of Mexican immigrants and Mexican Americans, as well as other immigrant groups in the United States, is one of violent conflict over the cultural, social, and political meanings of the American Dream. The meanings Mexican workers brought to California's fields hold a different set of keys to the doors of social justice.

APPENDIX

Repatriation Statistics and Tables

From repatriation statistics collected by the Mexican government, it is possible to create the following profile of Mexican immigrants who took part in formal repatriation from San Bernardino, Riverside, and San Diego counties.[1] Most repatriates traveled in family groups of more than three people, headed by men between the ages of thirty and forty-nine. The majority of spouses were in their twenties. Over half of the repatriates were children, and nearly two-thirds of children traveling with heads of household were under ten years of age. Few extended families participated in formal repatriation, which may reflect the type of households typical of the settled immigrant population.[2] Most repatriates listed towns and cities in the north-central states of Mexico as their destination. Repatriates destined for the same towns and cities traveled together. The majority of repatriates went to states in the north-central region of Mexico—Durango, Guanajuato, Jalisco, Michoacán, and Zacatecas—those states from which most immigration originated. The destinations of repatriates leaving from San Diego contrasted with this trend, as over half headed for border states. It is probable, given the policy of the Mexican government to move repatriates to the interior, that the destinations listed were transfer points rather than ultimate destinations.

Notes

1. See Tables 1–7.
2. Arnoldo de León found that the nuclear family prevailed among Mexican immigrants in Texas throughout the last half of the nineteenth century; *The Tejano Community, 1836–1900* (Albuquerque: University of New Mexico Press, 1982), 107; 128–129, table 18.

TABLE 1
SIZE OF REPATRIATE GROUPS TRAVELING TOGETHER FROM SAN BERNARDINO, RIVERSIDE, AND SAN DIEGO COUNTIES, 1931–1932

Number in group	Number of groups	Total number of individuals
1	763	763
2	225	450
3	191	573
4	147	588
5	141	705
6	117	702
7	96	672
8	59	472
9	29	261
10	16	160
11	9	99
12	5	60
13	2	26
	1,800	5,531

Missing cases: 9

TABLE 2
AGES OF REPATRIATES FROM SAN BERNARDINO AND
RIVERSIDE COUNTIES, 1931–1932

Age group	Number	Percent of total
0–9	922	34.9
10–19	383	14.5
20–29	418	15.8
30–39	406	15.4
40–49	242	9.2
50–59	123	4.7
60+	147	5.6
	2,641	100.0

Missing cases: 846

TABLE 3

AGE COHORT OF REPATRIATE FAMILIES FROM SAN BERNARDINO
AND RIVERSIDE COUNTIES, 1931–1932

	Head of household	Spouse	Child	Parent	Sibling	Other
0–9	0	0	587	0	1	10
%	0	0	66.9	0	6.3	30.3
10–19	12	9	230	0	5	6
%	1.5	4.2	26.2	0	31.3	18.2
20–29	192	94	42	0	4	5
%	24.0	43.5	4.8	0	25.0	15.2
30–39	258	60	11	0	5	0
%	32.2	27.9	1.3	0	31.3	0
40–49	167	23	6	1	1	4
%	20.8	10.7	.7	5.9	6.3	12.1
50–59	73	17	0	3	0	2
%	9.1	7.9	0	17.6	0	6.1
60 +	99	12	1	13	0	6
%	12.4	5.6	.1	76.5	0	18.2

Total: 1,959
Did not designate: 1,528

TABLE 4
DESTINATIONS OF REPATRIATES FROM SAN BERNARDINO,
RIVERSIDE, AND SAN DIEGO COUNTIES, 1931–1932

State in Mexico	San Bernardino and Riverside		San Diego	
	No.	%	No.	%
Aguascalientes	159	5.2	13	.7
Baja California	0	0	928	49.0
Chihuahua	345	11.4	122	6.0
Coahuila	287	9.4	45	2.4
Colima	2	.1	6	.3
Distrito Federal	66	2.2	47	2.5
Durango	175	5.8	30	1.6
Guanajuato	599	19.7	60	3.2
Guerrero	0	0	9	.5
Hidalgo	0	0	1	.1
Jalisco	352	11.6	107	5.7
Michoacán	533	17.5	56	3.0
Morelos	1	0	0	0
Nayarit	19	.6	16	.8
Nuevo León	20	.7	13	.7
Oaxaca	1	0	3	.2
Puebla	10	.3	0	0
Querétaro	2	.1	0	0
San Luis Potosí	2	.1	7	.4
Sinaloa	166	5.5	127	6.7
Sonora	96	3.2	259	13.7
Tamaulipas	3	.1	2	.1
Veracruz	3	.1	2	.1
Zacatecas	197	6.5	29	1.5
	3,038	100.0	1,893	100.0

Did not designate: 449 (San Bernardino); 20 (San Diego)

TABLE 5

SIZE OF REPATRIATE GROUPS TRAVELING TOGETHER FROM
SAN BERNARDINO AND RIVERSIDE COUNTIES, 1931–1932

Number in group	Number of groups	Number of individuals	Percent of total
1	423	423	12.1
2	139	278	8.0
3	100	300	8.6
4	86	344	9.8
5	96	480	13.8
6	76	456	13.1
7	65	455	13.0
8	41	328	9.4
9	22	198	5.7
10	11	110	3.2
11	6	66	1.9
12	3	36	1.0
13	1	13	0.4
	1,069	3,487	100.0

Missing cases: 0

TABLE 6

RELATIONSHIPS OF REPATRIATES TRAVELING IN GROUPS FROM
SAN BERNARDINO AND RIVERSIDE COUNTIES, 1931–1932,
DESIGNATED BY SEX

	Male	Female	Total	%
Head of household	945	56	1,001	44.6
Spouse	4	234	238	10.6
Child	506	429	935	41.7
Parent	4	13	17	0.8
Sibling	12	9	21	0.9
Other	12	20	32	1.4
	1,483	761	2,244	100.0

Did not designate: 1,243

TABLE 7
AGES OF REPATRIATES FROM SAN BERNARDINO AND
RIVERSIDE COUNTIES, 1931–1932

	Percent of total	Cumulative percent
0–12	41.7	41.7
13–20	8.8	50.5
21–30	17.3	67.8
31–40	14.6	82.4
41–50	8.3	90.7
51–60	5.2	95.9
60 +	4.1	100.0
	100.0	100.0

TABLE 8
SIZE OF REPATRIATE GROUPS TRAVELING TOGETHER FROM
SAN DIEGO COUNTY, 1931–1932

Number in group	Number of groups	Total number of individuals	Percent of total	Cumulative percent
1	209	209	34.8	34.8
2	86	172	14.3	49.2
3	91	273	15.2	64.3
4	61	244	10.2	74.5
5	45	225	7.5	82.0
6	41	246	6.8	88.8
7	31	217	5.2	94.0
8	18	144	3.0	97.0
9	7	63	1.2	98.2
10	5	50	.8	99.0
11	3	33	.5	99.5
12	2	24	.3	99.8
13	1	13	.2	100.0
	600	1,913	100.0	

Missing cases: 0

NOTES

Introduction

1. The terms *America* and *American* are not the exclusive property of the U.S. but also encompass countries in Latin America. When I refer to the American Revolution and the American Dream, I am invoking popularized terms that signify particular values, ideologies, and myths.

2. In this sense, the American Dream became fetishized, an object no longer responsive to interactions among people or between people and the world. Donna Haraway's discussion of the fetishization of science has had a great influence on my thinking about the American Dream. She writes: "we have granted science the role of a fetish, an object human beings make only to forget their role in creating it, no longer responsive to the dialectical interplay of human beings with the surrounding world in the satisfaction of social and organic needs." Donna Haraway, *Simians, Cyborgs, and Women: The Reinvention of Nature* (New York: Routledge, 1991), 8–9.

3. Lee Quinby writes of self-stylization as a "practice of freedom" and draws on Michel Foucault's "Technologies of the Self" to analyze a tradition of ethics in the United States in which the self is an "art of living and a style of liberty." Lee Quinby, *Freedom, Foucault, and the Subject of America* (Boston: Northeastern University Press, 1991), 3–4.

4. Stuart Hall, "Ethnicity: Identity and Difference," *Radical America*, 23, no. 4 (1990), 10–11. Hall discusses another

way the question of identity has been destabilized, in addition to conditions outside the self, the unconscious self, and language: the "relativization of the Western world—of the discovery of other worlds, other peoples, other cultures, and other languages" so that Western thought is seen "not as absolute, disinterested, objective, neutral, scientific, non-powerful truth, but dirty truth—truth implicated in the hard game of power" (p. 11).

5. Quinby examines Foucault's concept of technologies of normalization, defined in *Discipline and Punish: The Birth of the Prison* (New York: Vintage, 1979), as those forms of power that produce conformity through the regulation and disciplining of the body or soul, that categorize people as normal or abnormal, and that homogenize diverse peoples, repressing and erasing their difference through national identification or "eugenic obligation." Quinby, *Freedom, Foucault, and the Subject of America*, 4.

6. Quinby's discussion of pastoral ethics, which postulates an interiorist self that is revealed through communion with God, and of an ethics of human sciences that stresses a scientific molding of a biologically constructed self, as well as her analysis of a material, rational, imagined self, influenced my thinking about identity and the American Dream. Ibid., 7–9.

7. Haraway, *Simians, Cyborgs, and Women*, 7.

8. I am informed here by Quinby's discussion of a shift from a Gramscian critique of the totalizing concept of *the* revolution to Foucault's notion of resistances as strategies for change. Quinby, *Freedom, Foucault, and the Subject of America*, 13.

9. See Benedict Anderson's discussion of nations as invented (created) or imagined communities in *Imagined Communities, Reflections on the Origin and Spread of Nationalism*, rev. ed. (New York: Verso, 1991), 5–7.

10. This analysis draws from both Antonio Gramsci's concept of the organic intellectual and Michel Foucault's specific intellectual, offering a vision of possible social transformation through a variety of strategies that are, in Quinby's words,

"local, partial, and often contradictory." Quinby, *Freedom, Foucault, and the Subject of America*, 13. I am indebted to Robin D. G. Kelley and his brilliant theoretical essay, "'We Are Not What We Seem': Rethinking Black Working-Class Opposition in the Jim Crow South," *Journal of American History* 80, no. 1 (June 1993), 75–112, in which he lays out a research plan for looking at the ways hidden forms of resistance are made visible; how working-class consciousness is shaped by class, gender, and race; and how the gulf between the social and cultural world of working-class African-Americans and their political struggle might be bridged. His thoughts provided me with a way to look at the everyday lives of Mexican immigrants to discover the hidden forms of resistance in which they engaged. Kelley integrates the work of a number of thinkers and develops a way of interrogating experience that transcends these individual works: E. P. Thompson, *The Making of the English Working Class* (New York: Vintage Books, 1966); Michel de Certeau, *The Practice of Everyday Life* (Berkeley and Los Angeles: Univesity of California Press, 1984); and especially James C. Scott, *Domination and the Arts of Resistance: Hidden Transcripts* (New Haven, Conn.: Yale University Press, 1990).

11. Antonio Gramsci, *Gramsci's Prison Letters: A Selection*, trans. and intro. by Hamish Henderson (London: Zwan in association with the Edinburgh Review, 1988; *Letters from Prison, Selected*, trans. and intro. by Lynne Lawner (New York: Harper and Row, 1973); *An Antonio Gramsci Reader: Selected Writings, 1916–1935*, ed. David Forgacs (New York: Schocken Books, 1989); and *Selections from Political Writings, 1910–1920*, ed. Quintin Hoare; trans. John Mathews (Minneapolis: University of Minnesota Press, 1990). Edward Said's discussion of cultural hegemony and the strength and durability of the concept of Orientalism was very helpful to me in understanding the force of the American Dream in American thought. Edward Said, *Orientalism* (New York: Vintage Books, 1979), 6–7.

12. A number of books look at specific aspects of farm labor in California. Carey McWilliams, in *Factories in the Field: The Story of Migratory Farm Labor in California* (1939; rpt. Santa

Barbara, Calif.: Peregrine Publishers, 1971) describes the re-cruitment of immigrant farm labor. Cletis Daniel's *Bitter Harvest: A History of California Farmworkers, 1870–1941* (Ithaca, N.Y.: Cornell University Press, 1981) focuses on the exploit-ative nature of farm labor in California. Studies dealing with Mexican immigration include Lawrence Cardoso's *Mexican Emigration to the United States, 1897–1931* (Tucson: University of Arizona Press, 1980), Albert Camarillo's *Chicanos in a Changing Society: From Mexican Pueblos to American Barrios in Santa Barbara and Southern California, 1848–1930* (Cambridge, Mass.: Harvard University Press, 1979), Richard Griswold del Castillo's *The Los Angeles Barrio, 1850–1890: A Social History*, (Berkeley: University of California Press, 1979), and Ricardo Romo's *East Los Angeles: History of a Barrio* (Austin: University of Texas Press, 1983). Such studies focus either on the general process of immigration or on settlement of immigrants in par-ticular communities. Vicki L. Ruiz offers an insightful account of the strategies women developed to gain control over their own labor power in her study of agricultural workers in the canning industry, *Cannery Women, Cannery Lives: Mexican Women, Unionization, and the California Food Processing Industry, 1930–1950* (Albuquerque: University of New Mexico Press, 1987). David Montejano's *Anglos and Mexicans in the Making of Texas, 1836–1986* (Austin: University of Texas Press, 1987) and Dennis Valdes's *Al Norte: Agricultural Workers in the Great Lakes Region, 1917–1970* (Austin: University of Texas Press, 1991) lay crucial foundations for theorizing Mexican farm la-bor in the United States.

Chapter 1: Pastoral Dreams in California

1. Some writers have argued that the agrarian myth was replaced by "modern industrial values" in California. See Cletus Daniel, *Bitter Harvest: A History of California Farm Work-ers, 1870–1941* (Ithaca, N.Y.: Cornell University Press, 1981).
2. On republicanism, see Sean Wilentz, *Chants Democratic:*

New York City and the Rise of the American Working Class, 1788–1850 (New York: Oxford University Press, 1984). On the frontier myth, see Richard Slotkin, *The Fatal Environment: The Myth of the Frontier in the Age of Industrialization, 1800–1890* (New York: Athenaeum, 1985). Slotkin focuses on the frontier myth but makes some provocative suggestions about the tension between the material promise and spiritual threat of technological progress. The frontier myth receives its comeuppance in Patricia Nelson Limerick, *The Legacy of Conquest: The Unbroken Past of the American West* (New York: Norton, 1988). Limerick's insights on the way myth has been used to gain support for Western industrial development are invaluable.

3. Henry Nash Smith, *Virgin Land: The American West as Symbol and Myth* (Cambridge, Mass.: Harvard University Press, 1950), 259; Richard Hofstadter, *The Age of Reform* (New York: Knopf, 1955), 40; Leo Marx, *The Machine in the Garden: Technology and the Pastoral Ideal in America* (New York: Oxford University Press, 1964), 220, 364.

4. Paul S. Taylor, "Historical Background of California Farm Labor," *Rural Sociology* 1 (September 1936), 281–295.

5. Kevin Starr, *Inventing the Dream: California through the Progressive Era* (New York: Oxford University Press, 1985), 139.

6. Ibid., 46, 174–175.

7. Marx, *Machine in the Garden*, 3.

8. Between 1870 and 1940, California agriculture underwent a fundamental change in the kind of crops farmers grew and in the structure of agricultural production. By the turn of the century, this transition was well under way; in 1900, California stood in ninth place in the value of farm commodities produced (U.S. Bureau of the Census, *Twelfth Census* (1900), vol. 5, table 58, 703). By 1930, California had become one of the two leading agricultural states in the nation. California and Iowa tied for first place in total value of farm products in 1930. Clarke A. Chambers, *California Farm Organizations: A Historical Study of the Grange, the Farm Bureau, and the Associated*

Farmers, 1929–1941 (Berkeley: University of California Press, 1952), 2. Excellent soil conditions, irrigation projects, improved transportation networks, refrigerated railroad cars, and a factory system of farming contributed to the rapid development of California agriculture.

9. LaWanda Cox, "Agricultural Labor in the United States, 1865–1900, with Special Reference to the South," (Ph.D. diss., University of California, Berkeley, 1912), 12–13, 34, 37–38.

10. Carey McWilliams, *Factories in the Field: The Story of Migratory Farm Labor in California* (1939; rpt. Santa Barbara, Calif.: Peregrine Publishers, 1971), 56–57.

11. Ronald Takaki, *Strangers from a Different Shore: A History of Asian-Americans* (Boston: Little, Brown and Company, 1989), 15, 413.

12. Sucheng Chan, *This Bittersweet Soil: The Chinese in California Agriculture, 1860–1910* (Berkeley: University of California Press, 1986), 7.

13. Lucille Eaves, *A History of California Labor Legislation* (Berkeley: University of California Press, 1910), 107.

14. Chan, *This Bittersweet Soil*, 3.

15. Ibid., 2, 37.

16. Stuart Jamieson, *Labor Unionism in American Agriculture*, U.S. Department of Labor, Bureau of Labor Statistics (Washington: United States Government Printing Office, 1945), 31; *Pacific Rural Press* (June 30, 1877).

17. McWilliams, *Factories in the Field*, 75.

18. *Pacific Rural Press* (June 10, 1893).

19. Lawrence J. Jelinek, *Harvest Empire: A History of California Agriculture* (San Francisco: Boyd and Fraser Publishing Co., 1979), 53.

20. Eaves, *History of California Labor Legislation*, 135.

21. Chan, *This Bittersweet Soil*, 39–41.

22. McWilliams, *Factories in the Field*, 75–77; Takaki, *Strangers from a Different Shore*, 111; Chan, *This Bittersweet Soil*, 39–41; Ronald Takaki, *Iron Cages: Race and Culture in 19th-Century America* (New York: Oxford Univesity Press, 1990), 248; John

Higham, *Strangers in the Land: Patterns of American Nativism, 1860–1925* (New York: Atheneum, 1978) 18, 25, 167.

23. Eaves, *History of California Labor Legislation*, 137.

24. *Pacific Rural Press*, (June 30, 1877).

25. Chan, *This Bittersweet Soil*, 3, 41–42; Takaki, *Strangers from a Different Shore*, 14; Stanford M. Lyman, *Chinese Americans* (New York: Random House, 1974), 66.

26. Takaki, *Strangers from a Different Shore* 111–112; McWilliams, *Factories in the Field*, 74; Lyman, *Chinese Americans*, 66–67.

27. Federal Writers' Project Collection, "Oriental Labor Unions and Strikes," Bancroft Library, University of California, Berkeley, 8; California Bureau of Labor Statistics, *1st Biennial Report, 1884*; *9th Biennial Report, 1899–1900*, in Federal Writers' Project Collection, "Oriental Labor Unions and Strikes," 4.

28. McWilliams, *Factories in the Field*, 75.

29. *Pacific Rural Press* (March 3, 1894; May 24, 1894; August 18, 1894; November 17, 1894; and December 1, 1894).

30. Takaki, *Strangers from a Different Shore*, 29.

31. U.S. Bureau of the Census, *Twelfth Census* (1900), vol. 1, table 13, 487; *Fifteenth Census* (1930), vol. 3, table 17, 12.

32. McWilliams, *Factories in the Field*, 77, 105.

33. Sucheng Chan, *Asian Americans: An Interpretive History* (Boston: Twayne Publishers, 1991), 38, 87, 106; Chan, *This Bittersweet Soil*, 279; U.S. Congress, *Reports*, Senate Committee on Immigration, 1911, vol. 24, 20–33.

34. *Pacific Rural Press* (April 7, 1894), 264.

35. McWilliams, *Factories in the Field*, 108; Chan, *This Bittersweet Soil*, 77–78; Takaki, *Strangers from a Different Shore*, 46.

36. Yamato Ichihashi, *Japanese in the United States* (Stanford, Calif.: Stanford University Press, 1932), 172–176; McWilliams, *Factories in the Field*, 107.

37. Ichihashi, *Japanese in the United States*, 172–175, Jamieson, *Labor Unionism in American Agriculture*, 52.

38. Chan, *This Bittersweet Soil*, 37; Takaki, *Strangers from a Different Shore*, 189–190.

39. H. A. Millis, *The Japanese Problem in the United States* (New York: The McMillan Company, 1915), 111.

40. *Oakland Tribune* (April 1, 1903); Tomas Almaguer, "Racial Domination and Class Conflict in Capitalist Agriculture: The Oxnard Sugar Beet Workers' Strike of 1903," *Labor History* 25, no. 3 (Summer 1984), 342–343; McWilliams, *Factories in the Field*, 111.

41. Chan, *Asian Americans*, 37; Takaki, *Strangers from a Different Shore*, 180, 188–197; McWilliams, *Factories in the Field*, 112–113.

42. Chan, *Asian Americans*, 16, 38; Takaki, *Strangers from a Different Shore*, 27, 46, 203–208; Chan, *This Bittersweet Soil*, 38, 58.

43. U.S. Bureau of the Census, *Fifteenth Census*, (1930), vol. 3, table 2, 233.

44. Takaki, *Strangers from a Different Shore*, 15.

45. Ibid., 62.

46. Chan, *Asian Americans*, 4.

47. Brenda Sunoo, *Korean American Writings: Selected Material from Insight, Korean American Bimonthly* (New York, 1975), 25, quoted in Takaki, *Strangers from a Different Shore*, 273.

48. Chan, *Asian Americans*, 55; McWilliams, *Factories in the Field*, 116–122.

49. Bureau of the Census, *Fifteenth Census* (1930), vol. 3, table 2, 233; Takaki, *Strangers from a Different Shore*, 315.

50. Bruno Lasker, *Filipino Immigration to the Continental United States and to Hawaii* (Chicago: University of Chicago Press for the American Council, Institute of Pacific Relations, 1931), 204–211; Varden Fuller, "The Supply of Agricultural Labor as a Factor in the Evolution of Farm Organization in California" (Ph.D. diss., University of California, 1939), printed in Subcommittee of the U.S. Senate Committee on Education and Labor, Hearings on Violations of Free Speech and Rights of Labor, 76th Congress, 3d sess., pt. 54, 19857; Takaki, *Strangers from a Different Shore*, 57.

51. Jamieson, *Labor Unionism in American Agriculture*, 74–75.

52. Takaki, *Strangers from a Different Shore*, 321–324.
53. Ibid., 333; *Pacific Rural Press* (January 19, 1929), 72; (April 13, 1929), 476–477; (February 15, 1930), 209; Fuller, "Supply of Agricultural Labor," 19858.
54. Takaki, *Strangers from a Different Shore*, 331, 333.
55. Ibid., 333.
56. Growers were the principal proponents of the first Bracero Program, a federal program to recruit temporary workers from Mexico during World War I to do field labor. See Lawrence Cardoso, "Labor Emigration to the Southwest, 1916–1920," in *Mexican Workers in the United States*, ed. George C. Kiser and Martha Woody (Albuquerque: University of New Mexico Press, 1979).
57. The characterization of Mexican immigrants as "birds of passage" and the project of promoting this idea to the public is discussed at length in the correspondence of members of the Agricultural Department of the Los Angeles Chamber of Commerce and the San Joaquin Valley Labor Bureau; speeches and articles of the Commonwealth Club; and various news articles in the George Clements Collection, Graduate Research Library, University of California, Los Angeles.

Chapter 2: Mexican "Birds of Passage"

1. Oscar J. Martinez, "On the Size of the Chicano Population: New Estimates, 1850–1900," *Aztlan* 6, no. 1 (Spring 1975), 44–45, 56. Martinez estimates that between 87,000 and 117,000 Mexicans lived in the United States in 1850, 86,000 to 116,000 of them in the Southwest, and cites: Hubert H. Bancroft, *The Works of Hubert H. Bancroft* (San Francisco: A. L. Bancroft and Company, 1882–1890), vol. 16, 346; vol. 17, 342, 475; vol. 22, 642; U.S. Bureau of the Census, *Seventh Census of the United States* (1850); Terry G. Jordan, "Population Origins in Texas, 1850," *Geographical Review* 59 (1969): 83–103.
2. Official records show only 970 Mexican immigrants

entering the United States between 1894 and 1900; yet, during the ten-year period, 1890–1900, the Bureau of the Census counted an increase of 25,540 Mexican-born in the United States. The number of legal immigrants from Mexico did not exceed 330 in any given year for which immigrant officials kept records prior to 1901. So, if one allows 330 for each of the four years not recorded between 1890 and 1900 (1,320), only 2,290 of the 25,540 increase of Mexican-born in the United States are accounted for. This suggests that the remaining 23,250 emigrated by land. U.S. Department of the Treasury, Commissioner General of Immigration, *Annual Report, 1900*, 34–35, 37; U.S. Bureau of the Census, *Fifteenth Census* (1930), Population, vol. 2, 233.

3. The commissioner general of immigration reported that 486 Mexican immigrants entered the country in 1903. These were primarily skilled workers and professionals of the middle class. They had a total of $21,000 in their possession upon arrival, and all but fifty-eight of them were literate. The Bureau of Immigration listed only four as likely to become a public charge. The majority named coastal states as their final destination; 229 went to California and 148 to New York. Of the total, 132 were skilled workers. There were 17 professionals among the immigrants. Almost half (210) listed no occupation. Immigrants listing no occupation included women and children. The reported number of Mexican immigrants entering the United States in 1904, although more than double that for 1903, still was not significant. Immigrants entering in 1904 (1,009 in all) closely resembled those who came in 1903 in their occupations listed, money brought with them, literacy, and intended destination. U.S. Department of the Treasury, Commissioner General of Immigration, *Annual Report, 1903*, 18, 20, 22, 24, 26; U.S. Department of Commerce and Labor, Immigration and Naturalization Bureau, *Annual Report, 1904*, 5–7, 14–17. Census reports are of limited value because Mexican-born were not listed in a separate category.

4. Lawrence A. Cardoso, *Mexican Emigration to the United States, 1897–1931* (Tucson: University of Arizona Press, 1980), 2.

5. Ibid., 5–6.

6. George McCutchen McBride, *The Land Systems of Mexico* (New York: American Geographical Society, 1923), 75; Eyler N. Simpson, *The Ejido, Mexico's Way Out* (Chapel Hill: University of North Carolina Press, 1937), 28.

7. Helen Phipps, *Some Aspects of the Agrarian Question in Mexico: A Historical Study* (Austin: University of Texas Press, 1925), 110–111.

8. Simpson, *Ejido, Mexico's Way Out*, 29.

9. McBride, *Land Systems of Mexico*, 154. These states included Michoacán, Jalisco, Durango, Guanajuato, Zacatecas, and San Luis Potosí.

10. Cardoso, *Mexican Emigration to the United States*, 7.

11. Ibid., 10; Harry E. Cross and James Sandos, *Across the Border: Rural Development in Mexico and Recent Migration to the United States* (Berkeley: Institute of Governmental Studies, University of California, 1981), 5.

12. Cardoso, *Mexican Emigration to the United States*, 10.

13. Moises González Navarro, *La colonización en México, 1877–1910* (México: Talleres de Impresos de Estampillas y Valores, 1960), 132–136.

14. Arthur F. Corwin and Lawrence A. Cardoso, "Vamos al Norte: Causes of Mass Mexican Migration to the United States," in *Immigrants—and Immigrants: Perspectives on Mexican Labor Migration to the United States*, ed. Arthur F. Corwin, (Westport, Conn.: Greenwood Press, 1978), 28, 45.

15. Mark Reisler, *By the Sweat of their Brow: Mexican Immigrant Labor in the United States, 1900–1940* (Westport, Conn.: Greenwood Press, 1976), 5; Paul S. Taylor, "Historical Note on Dimmit County, Texas," *Southwestern Historical Quarterly* 34 (October 1930), 84.

16. U.S. Commissioner General of Immigration, *Annual Report 1900*, 38–39.

17. Ibid., 39; Federal Writers' Project, "The Contract Labor System in California Agriculture" (Oakland, Calif., n.d.), 38, Federal Writers' Project Collection, Bancroft Library, University of California, Berkeley.

18. F. W. Berkshire, supervising inspector, El Paso, Texas, to Commissioner General of Immigration, June 30, 1910, p. 7, Record Group (RG) 85, file 52546/31B, National Archives Record Service (NARS).

19. John R. Spencer, secretary-treasurer, Texas State Federation of Labor, to Frank Morrison, secretary of the American Federation of Labor, April 23, 1910, RG 85, file 52546/31A, NARS.

20. Frank Morrison to Commissioner General of Immigration, April 29, 1910, RG 85, file 52546/31A, NARS; Berkshire to Commissioner General, June 30, 1910, p. 2.

21. Federal Writers' Project, "Contract Labor System in California Agriculture," 38.

22. Report of Frank R. Stone to the Commissioner General of Immigration on activities of Labor Agents in Recruiting Mexican Labor, June 23, 1910 (hereafter referred to as Stone Report), RG 85, file 52546/31B, NARS. This in-depth study is a valuable source for the study of Mexican labor in the United States. It was first used in my dissertation, "Cycles of Immigration and Repatriation: Mexican Farm Workers in California Industrial Agriculture, 1900–1940" (Ph.D. diss., University of California at Riverside, 1985). More recently, see George J. Sanchez, *Becoming Mexican American: Ethnicity, Culture, and Identity in Chicano Los Angeles, 1900–1945* (New York: Oxford University Press, 1993).

23. Interviews of railroad conductors by Inspector Frank R. Stone, in Stone Report, RG 85, file 52546/31B, NARS.

24. Joseph S. Myers, immigration inspector, Section 24, El Paso, Texas, to Commissioner General of Immigration, Washington, D.C., January 9, 1914, p. 2, in Immigration and Naturalization Service files, RG 85, NARS.

25. Stone Report.

26. Interviews of Mexican farm workers, employers, railroad workers, ticket agents, and consuls by Inspector Frank R. Stone, in Stone Report.

27. Mario T. García, *Desert Immigrants: The Mexicans of El Paso, 1880–1920* (New Haven: Yale University Press, 1981), 35; Nathan L. Whetten, *Rural Mexico* (Chicago: University of Chicago Press, 1948), table 50, 261.

28. Stone Report.

29. Victor S. Clark, "Mexican Labor in the United States," *Bulletin of the Bureau of Labor* 17 (September 1908), 478–479.

30. Cardoso, *Mexican Emigration to the United States* 23.

31. Stone Report, 10.

32. Ibid., 21–23.

33. Ibid., 16.

34. Testimony of Delfino García, Macedonio Rodríguez, Santana Hernández, Jesus Elias, Gregorio Yslas, Marcos Yslas, Angel García, Regino Quesada, and Cruz Rodríguez at a meeting of the Special Board of Inquiry, held in the Office of the Supervising Inspector, El Paso, Texas, May 13, 1910, in Stone Report, exhibit 16.

35. Ibid., exhibit 17; Holmes Supply Company, Los Angeles, California, to J. W. Jenks, September 27, 1907, in Stone Report. The Holmes Supply Company, a commissary company that supplied workers to the Santa Fe Railroad, made the following promises when recruiting workers: (1) After one year of employment, the railroad would provide free passage to workers and their families at the rate of ½ cent per mile after three months employment for the company; (2) the railroad would provide free housing, fuel, and water; and (3) charges for supplies and board would not exceed fifty percent of workers' wages.

36. Stone Report, 26–27.

37. Ibid., 30.

38. Ibid., exhibit 11 and 12.

39. Investigation of Special Board of Inquiry, El Paso, Texas, by the Bureau of Immigration, Washington, D.C., 1911, RG 85, file 52546/31D, NARS.

40. Testimony of Juan Murillo, Special Board of Inquiry, Office of the Supervising Inspector, El Paso, Texas, May 28, 1910, in Stone Report, exhibit 14.

41. Ibid.

42. Ibid.

43. Testimony of Cirilio Curiél, Special Board of Inquiry, Office of the Supervising Inspector, El Paso, April 26, 1910, in Stone Report.

44. Interviews, representatives of the Garza Employment Agency, the Contreras and Sánchez Agency, and the B.B.B. Service, San Antonio, Texas, by Frank R. Stone, in Stone Report.

45. Interview, representatives of Contreras and Sánchez Agency, San Antonio, and Santiago, Hill and Company, Laredo, Texas, in Stone Report.

46. Henry Bamford Parkes, *A History of Mexico* (Boston: Houghton Mifflin Company, 1938), 385.

47. Secretaría de Industria de México, *La industria, el comercio y el trabajo en México*, 5 vols. (México: Tipografía. Galas, 1928), vol. 3, 64–65.

48. Cardoso, *Mexican Emigration to the United States* 88–89; Manuel Gamio, *Mexican Immigration to the United States: A Study of Human Migration and Adjustment* (Chicago: University of Chicago Press, 1928–1934).

49. Mexican Fact-Finding Committee, *Mexicans in California: Report of Governor C. C. Young's Mexican Fact-Finding Committee* (San Francisco: California State Printing Office, 1930; reprint ed., San Francisco: R&E Research Associates, 1970), 33–34; Varden Fuller, "The Supply of Agricultural Labor as a Factor in the Evolution of Farm Organization in California" (Ph.D. diss., University of California, 1939), printed in 76th Cong., 3d sess., S. Res. 226, U.S. Senate, Hearings before a Subcommittee on Education and Labor, Violations of Free Speech and Rights of Labor (La Follette Committee), pt. 54, 19852.

50. Lawrence Cardoso, "Labor Emigration to the Southwest, 1916–1920," in *Mexican Workers in the United States*, ed. George C. Kiser and Martha Woody (Albuquerque: University of New Mexico Press, 1979), 16.

51. Fuller, "Supply of Agricultural Labor," 19852; Cardoso, "Labor Emigration to the Southwest," 18.

52. Corwin and Cardoso, "Vamos al Norte," 52.

53. Cardoso, *Mexican Emigration to the United States*, 98–103.

54. Fuller, "Supply of Agricultural Labor," 19860.

55. Carey McWilliams, *Factories in the Field: The Story of Mi-*

gratory Farm Labor in California (1939; rpt. Santa Barbara, Calif.: Peregrine Publishers, 1971), 125. The census estimated that Mexican workers comprised only twenty-one percent of the total farm labor force, while farmers claimed they constituted over eighty percent of their workers. The lower census estimates result from the fact that the census was taken during the early spring, during the low point of agricultural employment. It is likely that many Mexican farm workers were not counted in the census because some had returned to Mexico and because a number had taken jobs in other industries, thus listing those jobs as their occupation.

56. Fuller, "Supply of Agricultural Labor," 19859.

Chapter 3: Whiteness and Ethnic Identity

1. F. W. Berkshire, supervising inspector, El Paso, Texas, to Commissioner General of Immigration, June 30, 1910, 3–5, Record Group (RG) 85, file 52546/31B, National Archives Record Service (NARS).

2. J. L. Hibbard to Holmes Supply Company, September 26, 1907, in Frank R. Stone, "Report to the Commissioner General of Immigration on Activities of Labor Agents in Recruiting Mexican Labor," June 23, 1910 (hereafter referred to as Stone Report), exhibit 24, RG 85, file 52546/31B, NARS.

3. Holmes Supply Company to J. W. Jenks, September 27, 1907, in Stone Report, exhibit 25.

4. Hibbard to Holmes Supply Company, September 26, 1907.

5. *Topeka State Journal*, August 14, 1913, RG 85 file 52546/31G, NARS. David Gordon, Richard Edwards, and Michael Reich, *Segmented Work, Divided Workers: The Historical Transformation of Labor in the United States* (Cambridge: Cambridge University Press, 1982) informs this analysis of the "stigmatization" of certain jobs through the association of these jobs with workers who have low status in American society: women, African Americans, and other people of color.

The low status of workers is transferred to the work they do, and other workers are reluctant (or refuse) to do such work.

6. *Santa Fe Magazine*, January 1914, 41–42, RG 85, file 52546/31G, NARS; A. A. Graham, attorney at Law, Topeka, Kansas, to the Honorable William P. Wilson, secretary of labor, Washington, D.C., January 17, 1914, RG 85, file 52546/31G, NARS.

7. U.S. Immigration Commission, *Reports of the Immigration Commission, Immigrants in Industries*, pt. 25, no. 3 (Washington, D.C.: Government Printing Office, 1911), 31.

8. Sworn statement of Joseph B. Donohue, Hanlin Supply Co., to Frank R. Stone, in the Office of the Supervising Inspector, El Paso, Texas, May 14, 1910, in Stone Report, exhibit 7, June 23, 1910; interview of N. B. Lautz, assistant to the general manager of the Eastern Grand Division of the Santa Fe Railroad Co., in Stone Report.

9. Carey McWilliams, *Factories in the Field: The Story of Migratory Farm Labor in California* (1939; rpt. Santa Barbara, Calif.: Peregrine Publishers, 1971), 117–118.

10. Lawrence J. Jelinek, *Harvest Empire: A History of California Agriculture* (San Francisco: Boyd and Fraser, 1979) 53.

11. Of these groups, only Mexican workers worked in family units. Interview, son of Wiley B. Giffen, owner of the Giffen Ranch, Mendota, California, September 7, 1928, "Field Notes for *Mexican Labor in the United States*" (hereafter referred to as "Field Notes") Paul S. Taylor Collection, Bancroft Library, University of California, Berkeley. Captain Y. L. Harvill, employment manager of the Columbia Steel Corporation in Pittsburg, California, commented that the steel industry gave the better paying jobs to whites, just as employers of farm workers did: "We don't pay the Mexicans different rates for the same work but we give the better jobs with tonnage pay and higher earnings generally to the whites." Interview, Captain Y. L. Harvill, "Field Notes."

12. Interview, Juan Estrada, in San Luis Pool Hall, El Centro, California, October 14, 1928, "Field Notes."

13. Interview, Mexican grape picker northeast of Fresno, September 5, 1928, "Field Notes."

14. Interview, H. W. Owen, Brentwood, California, September 4, 1928, "Field Notes."

15. Stone Report June 23, 1910.

16. Judith Fincher Laird, "Argentine, Kansas: The Evolution of a Mexican-American Community, 1905–1940" (Ph.D. diss., University of Kansas, 1975).

17. Sworn statement of Joseph B. Donahue, Hanlin Supply Company, Santa Fe Western Division, in the Office of the Supervising Inspector, El Paso, Texas, May 4, 1910, 2:30 p.m., in Stone Report, exhibit 7.

18. Stone Report, 74; interview, N.B. Lautz, in Stone Report, 79.

19. Stone Report.

20. Manuel Gamio, *Mexican Immigration to the United States: A Study of Human Migration and Adjustment* (Chicago: University of Chicago Press, 1928–1934), 39.

21. Interview, Mexican grape picker, northeast of Fresno, September 5, 1928, p. 1, "Field Notes."

22. Interview, Mr. Martínez, Clovis, California, September 5, 1928, p. 6, "Field Notes."

23. *Topeka State Journal*, August 14, 1913, clippings in RG 85, NARS.

24. Frank R. Stone, immigration inspector, Section 24, El Paso, Texas, in Stone Report.

25. Ibid.

26. Holmes Supply Company to Jenks, September 27, 1907.

27. Stone Report.

28. Ibid.

29. Interview, William M. Henry, local manager of the Holmes Supply Company, El Paso, Texas, May 14, 1910, Stone Report, exhibit 6, 10–11.

30. Ibid.

31. Stone Report; interview, Ernest M. Clark, May 23, 1910, in Stone Report exhibit 8, 14.

32. Department of Industrial Relations, Division of Housing, *Biennial Report, 1945–48*; Division of Immigration and Housing, *Annual Report*, 1926, 17.

33. Division of Immigration and Housing, *Annual Report, 1926*, 17.

34. A. D. Shamel, "Housing Employees of California's Citrus Ranches," *California Citrograph* (October 1918), 294.

35. Ibid. (February, 1918), 71.

36. Ibid. (March 1918), 96.

37. Ibid. (May 1918), 150–151.

38. Paul S. Taylor, *Mexican Labor in the United States: The Imperial Valley.* University of California Publications in Economics, vol. 6, no. 1 (Berkeley: University of California Press, 1928), 55.

39. Paul S. Taylor, visit to Imperial Valley, August 30, 1928, "Field Notes."

40. Interview at Mexican camp underneath eucalyptus trees, northeast of Fresno, "Field Notes."

41. Interview, Mr. Martínez, Clovis, California, September 5, 1928, "Field Notes."

42. Carleton Beals, *American Earth: The Biography of a Nation* (Philadelphia: J.P. Lippincott Co., 1939), 395.

43. Omar Mills, *Health Problems among Migratory Workers* (Washington, D.C.: Farm Security Administration, 1939), 3; State Rural Resettlement Administration, Statement in Support of Project to Establish Camps for Migrants in California, 1935.

44. Carey McWilliams, Testimony, September 25, 1940, 76th Cong., 3d sess., House of Representatives, *Hearings before the Select Committee to Investigate the Interstate Migration of Destitute Citizens* (Washington, D.C.: Government Printing Office, 1941), part 6, 2542.

45. Interview, Graciola Camacho, McCabe Night School, May 19, 1927, "Field Notes."

46. Interview, Mr. Martínez, Clovis, California, September 5, 1928, "Field Notes."

47. Interview, Abraham Chacón, Brawley, California, in Maldonado's pool room, 1928, "Field Notes."

48. Interview, Ricardo Portillo, Brawley, California, 1928, "Field Notes."

49. State Emergency Relief Administration, *Migratory Labor in California* (San Francisco: California State Printing Office, 1936), 38.

50. Mario T. García, *Desert Immigrants: The Mexicans of El Paso, 1880–1920* (New Haven: Yale University Press, 1981) 112, 132, 135.

51. Interview, three sons of Fernando Valenzuela, Fresno, 1928, "Field Notes."

52. Mark Reisler, *By the Sweat of their Brow: Mexican Immigrant Labor in the United States, 1900–1940* (Westport, Conn.: Greenwood Press, 1976), 114.

53. Interview, Texano woman, Biola, California, September 10, 1928, "Field Notes."

54. Ricardo Romo, *East Los Angeles: History of a Barrio* (Austin: University of Texas Press, 1983), pp. 72–78.

55. Interview, George P. Clements, El Paso, Texas, 1928, "Field Notes."

56. Interview, Edwin B. Tilton, assistant superintendent of schools, San Diego, California, 1928, "Field Notes."

57. Interview, Mrs. Rodrigo, California, 1928, "Field Notes."

58. Interview, Americanization teacher, Santa Ana, California, 1928, "Field Notes."

59. Interview, Juan Estrada, El Centro, October 14, 1928, "Field Notes."

60. Interview, son of Wiley B. Giffen, Giffen Ranch, Mendota, California, September 7, 1928, "Field Notes."

61. Interview, Edwin B. Tilton, assistant superintendent of schools, San Diego, California, 1928, "Field Notes."

62. Interview, Mexican grape picker, northeast of Fresno, September 5, 1928, "Field Notes."

63. Interview, Burbank school boy, on the road from Fresno, September 5, 1928, "Field Notes."

64. Interview, Luz Romero, Brawley, California, 1928, "Field Notes."

65. Interview, Mr. Martinez, Clovis, California, September 5, 1928, "Field Notes."

66. Mexican Fact-Finding Committee, *Mexicans in Califor-nia: Report of Governor C. C. Young's Fact-Finding Committee* (San Francisco: California State Printing Office, 1930; reprint ed., San Francisco: R&E Research Associates, 1970), 177–178.

67. Ibid., 223.

68. Romo, *East Los Angeles*, 149–150.

69. García, *Desert Immigrants*, 97, 107–108.

70. McWilliams, *Factories in the Field*, 159, 160–161.

71. Ibid., 158–159; Cletus Daniel, *Bitter Harvest: A History of California Farm Workers, 1870–1941* (Berkeley: University of California Press, 1931), 89.

72. Daniel, *Bitter Harvest*, 89–90.

73. McWilliams, *Factories in the Field*, 163.

74. Ernesto Galarza, U.S. Select Committee to Investigate the Interstate Migration of Destitute Citizens, *Hearings: Interstate Migration*, 76th Cong., 3d sess., 1941–1942, pt. 10, 3884.

75. Charles Wollenberg, "Huelga, 1928 Style: The Imperial Valley Cantaloupe Workers' Strike," *Pacific Historical Review* (February 1969), 48.

76. Interview, Elmer Heald, district attorney, Imperial County, 1928, "Field Notes."

77. Interview, Brawley, California, 1928, "Field Notes."

78. Wollenberg, "Huelga," 48; Reisler, *By the Sweat of their Brow*, 234–236; Daniel, *Bitter Harvest*, 108–109.

Chapter 4: "Mexicans Go Home!"

1. Other immigrants have repatriated with the aid of their home countries, but the Mexican repatriation programs of the 1930s were the first to be organized and sponsored by U.S. government agencies. Dino Cinel, *From Italy to San Francisco: The Immigrant Experience* (Stanford, Calif.: Stanford University Press, 1982), 1: Wilbur S. Shepperson, "British Backtrailers: Working Class Immigrants Return," and Theodore Saloutos, "Exodus U.S.A.," both in *In the Trek of the Immigrants*, ed. O.

Fritiof Ander (Rock Island, Ill.: Augustana College Library, 1964), 179, 197; Theodore Saloutos, *They Remember America: The Story of the Repatriated Greek-Americans* (Berkeley: University of California Press, 1956), vii.

2. Abraham Hoffman, *Unwanted Mexicans in the Great Depression: Repatriation Pressures, 1929–1939* (Tucson: University of Arizona Press, 1974). Hoffman's pathbreaking study of repatriation chronicled the establishment of repatriation programs and laid the groundwork for my examination of programs in San Bernardino, Riverside, and San Diego counties, and for my interrogation of authorities' assertions that they were organizing the removal of foreigners without right to unemployment relief.

3. R. Reynolds McKay, "Texas Mexican Repatriation during the Great Depression" (Ph.D. diss., University of Texas, Austin, 1982), v; Paul S. Taylor, *Mexican Labor in the United States*, vol. 3, *Mexican Migration Statistics*, University of California Publications in Economics, vol. 12, no. 3 (Berkeley: University of California Press, 1934), table 8, 46–47.

4. U.S. Department of Commerce, Bureau of Foreign and Domestic Commerce, *Statistical Abstract of the United States* (Washington, D.C.: Government Printing Office, 1931), 365.

5. A total of 8,335 Mexicans were deported in the fiscal year ending June 30, 1930. U.S. Commissioner General of Immigration, *Annual Report, 1931*, 182–183, table 56.

6. Reports of American Consuls to the Secretary of State, Record Group (RG) 59, file 311.1215, National Archives Record Service (NARS); letters and reports from Mexican Consuls in Mexico City, Archivo de la Secretaría de Relaciones Exteriores (AREM), "Repatriation" files.

7. Robert S. Allen, "One of Mr. Hoover's Friends," *American Mercury* 35 (January 1932), 54.

8. Gardner Jackson, "Doak the Deportation Chief," *The Nation* (March 18, 1931), 295–296.

9. National Commission on Law Observance and Enforcement, *Report on the Enforcement of the Deportation Laws of the*

United States (Washington, D.C.: Government Printing Office, 1931), 177.

10. Commissioner General of Immigration, *Annual Report, 1931*, 35.

11. Ruben Oppenheimer, "The Deportation Terror," *The New Republic* (January 13, 1932), 232.

12. C. P. Visel to Col. Arthur M. Woods, January 6, 1931, in Clements Collection, box 80, Research Library, University of California, Los Angeles (hereafter referred to as Clements Collection).

13. C. P. Visel to Crime and Unemployment Committee, Los Angeles Chamber of Commerce, January 7, 1931, Clements Collection, box 80.

14. C. P. Visel to Secretary of Labor William S. Doak, January 11, 1931, Clements Collection, box 80.

15. Secretary of Labor William S. Doak to C. P. Visel, January 12, 1931, Clements Collection, box 80.

16. "Visel's Plan," carbon copy of transcript in Clements Collection, box 80.

17. C. P. Visel to Col. Arthur M. Woods, January 19, 1931, Clements Collection, box 80.

18. Press release, January 24, 1931, Clements Collection, box 80.

19. Memorandum to W. G. Arnoll from George P. Clements, January 31, 1931, Clements Collection, box 80.

20. George P. Clements to W. G. Arnoll, January 31, 1931, Clements Collection, box 80.

21. Thomas J. Maleady, American vice-consul in Mexico City to the Secretary of State of the United States, May 12, 1932, RG 59, file 311.1215/33, NARS.

22. Repatriation files, AREM.

23. Mexican families, including those headed by Mexican-descended American citizens and Mexican immigrants, received 24.5 percent of county relief for the indigent. Since only 9 to 11 percent of Mexican families receiving relief were headed by Mexican-born people, Mexican immigrant families amounted to only 2.5 percent of all relief cases. The remain-

ing 22 percent were Mexican American families. Hoffman, *Unwanted Mexicans in the Great Depression*, 86.

24. Mexican Fact-Finding Committee, *Mexicans in California: Report of Governor C. C. Young's Fact-Finding Committee* (hereafter referred to as *Governor Young Report*) (San Francisco: California State Printing Office, 1930; reprint ed., San Francisco: R&E Research Associates, 1970), 175, 191–192; Hoffman, *Unwanted Mexican Americans in the Great Depression*, 86.

25. Hoffman, *Unwanted Mexicans in the Great Depression*, 86. I am indebted to Hoffman's skillful description of the repatriation programs in California during the 1930s. This analysis is meant to expand on Hoffman's work by problematizing the explanations that program organizers gave for expelling Mexican immigrants and instigating a program to terrorize Mexican immigrants and Mexican Americans into leaving. In the following chapter, I expand further on Hoffman's study by looking at the complex role played by employers of farm workers.

26. *Governor Young Report*, 191. In San Diego and San Joaquin counties, the percentage of relief funds given to Mexican families was 1.5 percent higher than the percentage of total relief cases who were Mexican American. *Governor Young Report*, 196.

27. Ibid., 195–196.

28. Ibid., 196.

29. Mexican Americans and Mexican immigrants receiving relief numbered fewer than four thousand. Repatriation files, AREM.

30. Hoffman, *Unwanted Mexican Americans in the Great Depression*, 50, 87.

31. Ibid., 93.

32. Ibid., 87.

33. Ibid., 172, appendix C.

34. This may be because families with dependent children found it easier to establish their inability to pay full fares than did those without dependents. The Mexican Consulate required that repatriates establish financial need in order to

qualify for reduced or free passage on special repatriation trains.

35. Telegram to the Secretaria de Relaciones Exteriores (SRE) from Armando Alatorre, Mexican consul, San Bernardino, California, April 23, 1931, file IV-362-46, 1, Archivo de la Secretaria de Relaciones Exteriores (AREM).

36. Telegram to SRE from Alatorre, May 11, 1931 and repatriation lists, file IV-362-46, 12–20, AREM; appendix, table 4.

37. Mercedes Carreras de Velasco analyzes the role of the Mexican government in the repatriation of Mexican immigrants in *Los Mexicanos que devolvió la crisis, 1929–1932* (Tlateloco, México, D.F.: Secretaria de Relaciones Exteriores, 1974).

38. File IV-362-46, 84, AREM.

39. Telegram to SRE from Alatorre, June 21, 1931, and July 22, 1931, file IV-362-46, 29–32; AREM.

40. Repatriation list, file IV-362-46, 56, AREM.

41. Telegram to SRE from Alatorre, file IV-362-46, 33, AREM.

42. File IV-362-46, AREM.

43. Telegram from Consul Enrique Ferreira to SRE, April 22, 1931, file IV-360-38, 1, AREM.

44. Telegram from Ferreira to SRE, June 24, 1931, file IV-360-38, AREM.

45. Telegram from SRE to Ferreira, June 27, 1931, file IV-360-38, 7, AREM.

46. Report from Ferreira to SRE, July 17, 1931, file IV-360-38, 24–29, AREM.

47. Ibid., 25.

48. Ferreira to SRE, August 10, 1931, file IV-360-38, 31, 36, AREM.

49. Ibid., 36.

50. *Governor Young Report*, 196; Repatriation files, AREM.

51. Armando Amador, Mexican consul, San Diego, Cali-

fornia, to Secretaria de Relaciones Exteriores (SRE), March 17, 1932, file IV-360-38, 32, AREM.

52. File IV-36-0-38, 122, AREM.

53. Form found in file IV-360-38, AREM.

54. Report to SRE from Amador, September 3, 1932, file IV-360-38, 118–121, AREM.

55. Report to SRE, May 24, 1933, file IV-362-46, 289, AREM.

56. Departamento Consular to C. Consul de México, Los Angeles, January 12, 1932, file IV-357-13, 649, AREM; Fernando Alatorre, Mexican consul in San Bernardino to SRE, January 22, 1932, file IV-367-13, AREM.

57. Ibid.

58. Letters from Ferrocarriles Nacionales de México to SRE, December 31, 1931, file IV-362-46, 197, 203, 205, AREM.

59. Jimeno Hernandez, Aguascalientes, Mexico to S. F. Holcomb, Jr., San Diego, September 27, 1932, file IV-360-38, 156, AREM.

60. S. F. Holcomb, Jr., San Diego, to the Mexican consul in San Diego, October 11, 1932, file IV-360-38, 156, AREM.

61. Taylor, *Mexican Labor in the United States*, vol. 4, *Migration Statistics*, 46–47; Hoffman, *Unwanted Mexican Americans in the Great Depression*, 120.

62. U.S. Bureau of the Census, *Fifteenth Census* (1930), Population, vol. 2, 35, table 11.

63. "Repatriación de mexicanos en Detroit," file IV-350-44, AREM.

64. "Repatriaciones de mexicanos en Galveston," file IV-356-15, AREM; "Repatriaciones de mexicanos en Nueva York," file IV-359-58, AREM.

65. *El Porvenir*, November 12, 1931, clipping in RG 59, file 311.1215/27, NARS.

66. Romeyn Wormuth, American consul, to Secretary of State, November 12, 1932, RG 59, file 311.1215/37, NARS.

67. William P. Blocker, American consul, to the Secretary of State, January 2, 1932, RG 59, file 311.1215/30, NARS.

Chapter 5: Los Repatriados

1. National Department of Statistics, Mexico, Robert E. Cummings, acting military attaché to the chief of staff, Military Intelligence Division, War Department, Record Group (RG) 59, file 311.1215/42, National Archives Record Service (NARS); Thomas J. Maleady, vice consul, Mexico City, RG 59, file 311.1215/33, NARS.

2. American Consul Richard F. Boyce, report to secretary of state, "Repatriation of Mexicans through Laredo, Texas," January 8, 1931, RG 59, Department of State, file 311.1215/18, NARS.

3. Ibid.

4. Ibid.

5. Ibid., February 16, 1931, file 311.1215/20.

6. Ibid., October 17, 1931, file 311.1215/25, NARS. He based his conclusion on conversations with thousands of visa applicants, observations of Mexican residents in Texas, and articles by Paul S. Taylor.

7. Samuel Sokobin, American consul, Saltillo, Coahuila, November 5, 1931, RG 59, file 311.1215/26, NARS.

8. Edward I. Nathan, American consul in Monterrey, to Secretary of State, November 12, 1931, RG 59, file 311.1214/27, NARS.

9. *El Porvenir*, November 2, 1931, clipping found in RG 59, file 311.1215/27, NARS.

10. *El Porvenir*, November 12, 1931, clippings in RG 59, file 311.1215/27; Edward I. Nathan, American consul, Monterrey, Coahuila, November 12, 1931, RG 59, file 311.1215/27; *El Porvenir*, November 15, 1931, clipping in RG 59, file 311.1215/29, NARS.

11. George P. Clements, Clements Collection, box 80, Research Library, University of California, Los Angeles.

12. John Stockton Littel, vice-consul, Mexico City, to Secretary of State, April 26, 1932, RG 59, file 311.1215/32, NARS.
13. R. Reynolds McKay, "Texas Mexican Repatriation during the Great Depression" (Ph.D. diss., University of Texas, Austin, 1982), 494, 499.
14. James Gilbert, "A Field Study in Mexico of the Mexican Repatriation Movement," (M.A. thesis, University of Southern California, 1934), 106.
15. Ibid., 107.
16. Ibid., 108–109.
17. Ibid., 110.
18. Ibid., 113; McKay, "Texas Mexican Repatriation," 496–497; *El Continental*, El Paso, March 10, 1931; *La Prensa*, San Antonio, March 1931.
19. Gilbert, "Field Study in Mexico," 115.
20. Ibid., 113–114; Mercedes Carreras de Velasco, *Los mexicanos que devolvio la crisis, 1929–1932* (Tlateloco, México, D.F.: Secretaría de Relaciones Exteriores, 1974), 123; RG 59, file 812.61/49, NARS; file 812.6113/134, NARS; *Laredo Times*, January 30, 1930; *Eagle Pass Daily Guide*, May 11, 1931.
21. *La Prensa*, San Antonio, November 15, 1931.
22. McKay, "Texas Mexican Repatriation," 505–508.
23. Carreras de Velasco, *Los mexicanos que devolvio la crisis*, 124; McKay, "Texas Mexican Repatriation," 509.
24. Gilbert, "A Field Study in Mexico" 91.
25. Ibid., 92–93, 101.
26. Ibid., 96.
27. RG 59, file 812.5511/102, NARS; McKay, "Texas Mexican Repatriation," 518.
28. Gilbert, "Field Study in Mexico," 127.
29. Gilbert, "Field Study in Mexico," 130.
30. Gilbert, "A Field Study in Mexico," 137.
31. Interview, Arandas, Jalisco, quoted in Paul S. Taylor, *A Spanish–Mexican Peasant Community: Arandas in Jalisco* (Berkeley: University of California Press, 1933), 57.
32. Gilbert, "A Field Study in Mexico," 151.
33. Ibid.

34. Emory S. Bogardus, "Mexican Repatriates," *Sociology and Social Research* 17 (July–August 1933), 545–550.

35. Gilbert, "Field Study in Mexico" 140.

36. Ibid., 152.

37. Ibid., 156.

38. Interview, Arandas, Jalisco, quoted in Taylor, *Spanish-Mexican Peasant Community*, 61.

39. Emma R. Stevenson, "The Emigrant Comes Home," *Survey* 66 (May 1, 1931), 176.

40. Gilbert, "Field Study in Mexico," 164.

41. Abraham Hoffman, *Unwanted Mexicans in the Great Depression: Repatriation Pressures, 1929–1939* (Tucson: University of Arizona Press, 1974), 32, 116.

Chapter 6: Class War in the Fields

1. A total of 92,521 people were repatriated during these years. Mexican Migration Service, Record Group (RG) 59, file 811.111, Mexico Reports, 59, 80, 99, 122, 141, 142, National Archives Record Service (NARS).

2. U.S. Bureau of the Census, *Fifteenth Census* (1930), Population, vol. 2, 236.

3. U.S. Bureau of the Census, *Sixteenth Census* (1940), Population, vol. 2, 233.

4. James N. Gregory, *American Exodus: The Dust Bowl Migration and Okie Culture in California* (New York: Oxford University Press, 1989), 62.

5. Albert Croutch, "Housing Migratory Agricultural Workers in California, 1913–1948" (M.A. thesis, University of California, Berkeley, 1948), 46.

6. Newsclipping in Clements Collection, box 80, Graduate Research Library, University of California, Los Angeles.

7. *Douglas Daily Dispatch*, May 13, 1931, in files of the Department of State, RG 59, file 311.1215/22 NARS; Lewis V. Boyle, American consul, Agua Prieta, Mexico, to the Secretary of State, May 13, 1931, RG 59, file 311.1215/22, NARS.

8. *Douglas Daily Dispatch*, May 13, 1931.

9. Letter from Arthur G. Arnoll to Charles P. Visel, January 8, 1931, Clements Collection, box 80.

10. Arthur G. Arnoll to George P. Clements, February 25, 1931, Clements Collection, box 80.

11. Clarence H. Matson to Immigration Committee, April 25, 1931, Clements Collection, box 80; Matson to Rafael de la Colina, Mexican consul, April 25, 1931, Clements Collection, box 80.

12. Eugene Overton to the Board of Directors, Los Angeles Chamber of Commerce, May 6, 1931, Clements Collection, box 80.

13. *Los Angeles Evening Express* to Mr. J.A.H. Kerr, president, Los Angeles Chamber of Commerce, May 11, 1931, acknowledging receipt of a letter from the Chamber of Commerce, Clements Collection, box 80; memorandum from Bruce A. Findlay, manager, Exploitation and Public Relations Department, Los Angeles Chamber of Commerce, to Arthur G. Arnoll, May 15, 1931, regarding statement in *La Opinión* about Chamber's stance on expulsion of Mexican immigrants, Clements Collection, box 80.

14. Bruce A. Findlay to Lewis Weiss, manager, KHJ Radio Station, May 14, 1931, Clements Collection, box 80; Findlay to Glenn Rice, manager, KMPC Radio Station, May 15, 1931, Clements Collection, box 80.

15. Stuart Jamieson, *Labor Unionism in American Agriculture*, U.S. Department of Labor, Bureau of Labor Statistics, Bulletin no. 836 (Washington, D.C.: U.S. Government Printing Office, 1945), 80.

16. Ibid., 103.

17. Ibid., 90; memorandum from Mr. Gast to George P. Clements, "Berry Pickers' Strike," June 27, 1933, Clements Collection, box 80.

18. Jamieson, *Labor Unionism in American Agriculture*, 90–91.

19. Ibid., 92.

20. Memorandum from George P. Clements to Arthur G. Arnoll, July 20, 1933, Clements Collection, box 80.

21. Clements to Arnoll, July 12, 1933, Clements Collection, box 80.

22. California Superior Court, case 306101, complaint signed by David C. Marcus, attorney for plaintiffs, in Clements Collection, box 80.

23. Clements to Arnoll, July 20, 1933.

24. George P. Clements to Francisco Palomares, July 13, 1933, Clements Collection, box 80.

25. George P. Clements to Arthur G. Arnoll, July 13, 1933, Clements Collection, box 80. Graduate Research Library, University of California, Los Angeles.

26. Arnoll to Clements, July 27, 1933, Clements Collection, box 80.

27. Clements to Arnoll, July 20, 1933. This is a report of events in early July, Clements Collection, box 80.

28. Clements to Arnoll, July 12, 1933, Clements Collection, box 80.

29. Clements to Arnoll, July 17, 1933, Clements Collection, box 80.

30. Clements to Arnoll, July 20, 1933, Clements Collection, box 80.

31. Ibid. Reference to this meeting is made in a memorandum from Clements to Arnoll, July 25, 1933, Clements Collection, box 80.

32. Confidential report, July 19, 1933, Clements Collection, box 80.

33. Clements to Arnoll, July 25, 1933, Clements Collection, box 80.

34. Mark Reisler, *By the Sweat of their Brow: Mexican Immigrant Labor in the United States, 1900–1940* (Westport, Conn.: Greenwood Press, 1976), 228.

35. State Relief Administration, *Migratory Labor in California* (San Francisco: California State Printing Office, 1936), 109, 123; U.S. Bureau of Labor Statistics, *Monthly Labor Review* 49 (July 1939), 69; U.S. Bureau of the Census, *Historical Statistics of the United States* (Washington, D.C., 1960), 166; Varden Fuller, "The Supply of Agricultural Labor as a Factor in the

Evolution in Farm Organization," table 37, in La Follette Committee *Hearings*, pt. 54, 19890; Jamieson, *Labor Unionism in American Agriculture*, 80; U.S. Department of Agriculture, Bureau of Agricultural Economics, "The Agricultural Situation," vol. 17, no. 6 (June 1, 1933), 13, and no. 7 (July 1, 1933), 2.

36. Enrique A. Gonzales to Secretary Manuel Tellez, January 1, 1932, file 41-26-139, Archivo Relaciones Exteriores de México (AREM); Enrique Santibañez to all consuls, October 27, 1930, file 73-84-1, AREM; Enrique A. Gonzales to President Pascual Ortiz Rubio, April 4, Ortiz Rubio papers, Departmento de Gobernación, Archivo Nacional de México, Lecumberri, México, D.F.

37. Harold Fields, "Where Shall the Alien Work?" *Social Forces* 12 (December 1933), 213–214.

38. U.S. Department of Agriculture, "Agricultural Situation," vol. 17, no. 5 (May, 1, 1933), 1–3.

39. Fuller, "Supply of Agricultural Labor," 19890; Jamieson, *Labor Unionism in American Agriculture*, 80.

40. Quoted in Jamieson, *Labor Unionism in American Agriculture*, 103.

41. Jamieson, *Labor Unionism in American Agriculture*, 102–103.

42. Cletus Daniel, *Bitter Harvest, A History of California Farm Workers, 1870–1941* (Ithaca, N.Y.: Cornell University Press, 1981), 195–196; Jamieson, *Labor Unionism in American Agriculture*, 102.

43. *Los Angeles Times*, October 11, 1933; *New York Times*, October 22, 1933; Joan London and Henry Anderson, *So Shall Ye Reap* (New York: Crowell, 1977), 30; Daniel, *Bitter Harvest*, 216; Reisler, *By the Sweat of their Brow*, 241.

44. The ten major financial contributors to the organization were: the Southern Pacific Railroad; the Atcheson, Topeka, and Santa Fe Railroad; the Pacific Gas and Electric Company; the San Joaquin Cotton Oil Company; the Holly Sugar Corporation; the Spreckels Investment Company; the Canners' League; the Dried Fruit Association of California;

and the Industrial Association of San Francisco. Clarke Chambers, *California Farm Organizations: A Historical Study of the Grange, the Farm Bureau, and the Associated Farmers, 1929–1941* (Berkeley: University of California Press, 1952), 39–45.

45. Daniel, *Bitter Harvest*, 227–228.

46. Ibid., 228–229.

47. Ibid.

48. Campbell MacCulloch, "Labor Conditions in Imperial Valley," January 19, 1934, Records of the National Labor Relations Board, Region IX, RG 25, NARS.

49. Jamieson, *Labor Unionism in American Agriculture*, 108.

50. Chambers, California Farm Organizations, 70.

51. *New York Times*, January 20, 1935.

52. U.S. Senate, *Hearings* before a Subcommittee of Education and Labor, Violations of Free Speech and Rights of Labor (hereafter referred to as La Follette Committee, *Hearings*), 76th Cong., 3d sess., S. Res. 226, pt. 62, 22638; U.S. Department of Agriculture, Production and Marketing Administration, Labor Branch, Foreign and Domestic Agricultural Workers, *Special Report*, March 1, 1946, 3.

53. Jerold S. Auerbach discusses the La Follette Committee's formation, the mandate by Congress, and the ensuing investigations conducted by the committee in *Labor and Liberty: The La Follette Committee and the New Deal* (Indianapolis: Bobbs-Merrill Co., 1966).

54. Quoted in Auerbach, *Labor and Liberty*, 178.

55. John Steinbeck, *The Grapes of Wrath* (New York: Viking Press, 1939); Carey McWilliams, *Factories in the Field: the Story of Migratory Farm Labor in California* (1939; rpt. Santa Barbara: Peregrine Publishers, 1971). McWilliams completed his study in 1935, but did not publish it until 1939.

56. *New York Times*, December 5, 1939, 9. The committee listened to testimony in Los Angeles for twenty-eight days during December 1939 and January 1940, and in Washington, D.C., between May 2 and June 4, 1940, amassing evidence that workers in nearly every industry in the United States had been the targets of oppressive labor practices, New

York *Times*, December 19, 1939, 18; December 22, 1939, 20; December 24, 1939, IV, 6; May 28, 1940, 18.

57. La Follette Committee, *Hearings*, pt. 54, 19947.

58. Ibid., 178–180.

59. La Follette Committee, *Senate Report*, no. 1150, pt. 2, 64.

60. La Follette Committee, *Hearings*, pt. 53, 19692, 19696.

61. Ibid.

62. *Farm Tenancy Report of the President's Committee*, prepared under the auspices of the National Resources Committee (Washington, D.C., February 1937), 5.

63. Jamieson, *Labor Unionism in American Agriculture*, 16–18.

64. La Follette Committee, *Hearings*, pt. 49, 17938; Sidney C. Sufrin, "Labor Organization in Agricultural America, 1930–1935," *American Journal of Sociology* (January 1938), 554; Jamieson, *Labor Unionism in American Agriculture*, 17–18; La Follette Committee, *Hearings*, pt. 47, 17212; Chambers, *California Farm Organizations*, 39, 58.

65. La Follette Committee, *Hearings*, pt. 49, 17938.

66. Ibid.

67. Ibid., 19982.

68. Ibid.

69. Katherine Douglas, "West Coast Inquiry," *Survey Graphic* (April 1940), 229; Carey McWilliams, "Civil Rights in California," *New Republic* (January 22, 1940), 110; La Follette Committee, *Hearings*, pt. 47, 17332.

70. Jamieson, *Labor Unionism in American Agriculture*, 102, 111.

71. U.S. Senate, Subcommittee of the Committee on Education and Labor, *Hearings on S.1970*, 15, 40; *Congressional Record*, 76th Cong., 3d sess., May 20, 1939, 6375.

72. Letter to Elbert D. Thomas, chairman, Senate Committee on Education and Labor, ibid.

73. *Congressional Record*, 1st sess., vol. 84, pt. 3, March 28, 1939, 3395.

74. Auerbach, *Labor and Liberty*, 198.

75. *Congressional Record*, 1st sess., vol. 84, pt. 3, March 28, 1939, 3397.

76. Ibid.

77. Ibid., 3395.

78. *New York Times*, December 5, 1939, 9; December 8, 1939, 4; December 19, 1939, 18; December 22, 1939, 20; December 24, IV, 1939, 6; January 7, 1940, 6; January 16, 1940, 16; January 17, 1940, 15; January 25, 1940, 12; January 26, 1940, 15; January 27, 1940, 6; January 28, 1940, 1; January 29, 1940, 4; January 30, 1940, 3; March 4, 1940, 9; March 5, 1940, 25; March 7, 1940, 25; March 9, 1940, 17; March 6, 1940, 22; April 24, 1940, 15; May 3, 1940, 36; May 28, 1940, 18.

79. *Congressional Record*, 76th Cong., 3d sess., 1940, 6365; William E. Leuchtenburg, *Franklin D. Roosevelt and the New Deal* (New York: Harper and Row, 1963), 299.

80. *Congressional Record*, 76th Cong., 3d sess., 1940, 6696, 6699.

81. Ibid., 6365–6367; 6705, 6879, 6885, 6891.

82. Ibid.

83. Ibid.

84. While George conceded that "the Supreme Court have [*sic*] held . . . that the man who plants the seed and cultivates the tree which subsequently enters into commerce is engaged in interstate commerce," he maintained that the bill set "the precedent of prosecuting a man who plants a seed and cultivates a seed on the broad untenable theory that the tree or lumber from it may sometime enter into interstate commerce." *Congressional Record*, 76th Cong., 3d sess., 1940, p. 6697.

85. Ibid.

86. Ibid., 6879, 6900.

87. Ibid., 6904; Auerbach, *Labor and Liberty*, 203.

88. Ibid.

89. Harry A. Millis and Emily Clark Brown, *From the Wagner Act to Taft-Hartley: A Study of National Labor Policy and Labor Relations* (Chicago: University of Chicago Press, 1950), 271.

90. *Congressional Record*, 77th Cong., 2d sess., 1942, vol. 88, 3308–3314; *New York Times*, April 4, 1942; Millis and Brown, *From the Wagner Act to Taft-Hartley*, 271, 354; Christopher L. Tomlins, *The State and the Unions: Labor Relations, Law, and the Organized Labor Movement in America, 1880–1960* (Cambridge: Cambridge University Press, 1985), 266, 288.

91. A secondary boycott referred to the boycotting of businesses manufacturing or distributing boycotted products. Tomlins, *The State and the Unions*, 288.

92. Benedict Anderson, *Imagined Communities: Reflections on the Origin and Spread of Nationalism*, rev. ed. (London: Verso Press, 1991).

INDEX

Acapulco, Mexico, 103
African Americans, 161n5. *See also*
  farm workers, African American; workers: African American
agrarian ideal, 7–8, 13–14, 45,
  150n1. *See also* family farm,
  myth of the; pastoral ideal
agrarian reform (Mexico), 82
agricultural colonies (Mexico), 28,
  99, 102–106, 118–119
Agricultural Labor Relations
  Board, 137
agricultural workers. *See* farm
  workers
agriculture. *See* California: agricultural labor relations; crops;
  employers, agricultural; farming; growers; industrialized
  agriculture; labor supply
Aguascalientes, Mexico, 108
Alabama, 57
Alatorre, Fernando, 90–91
Albuquerque, N.M., 38
Alien Land Law of 1913 (California), 16, 20, 21, 24
aliens, Mexicans as, 81, 82, 137,
  167n2
Amador, Armando C., 89–90
American Dream: access to, 5–6,
  23; in California, 11; consequences of, 2, 11, 136;

contestation over, 3, 138; and
  cultural hegemony, 149n11;
  fetishization of, 147n2; and
  Mexican repatriates, 97;
  racialized nature of, 98; role of
  farming images in, 23; and self-
  hood, 148n6; social construction
  of, 2–8; use of term "American"
  in, 147n1
American Federation of Labor
  (AFL), 32, 123–124
American Fruit and Steamship
  Corporation, 93
American Latin League, 61
American Legionnaires, 123
American past, mythic, 12. *See also*
  agrarian ideal; frontier myth
Americanism, 12
Americanization, 46
Anaheim, Calif., 18, 58
Anderson, Benedict, 138
Anglo Americans, 25, 39–40. *See*
  also farm workers, Anglo American
anti-Chinese agitation, 17–18. *See*
  also immigrants, Chinese
anti-Filipino agitation, 22. *See also*
  immigrants, Filipino
anti-Japanese agitation, 20. *See also*
  immigrants, Japanese
Argentine (Kansas City, Mo.), 56

haciendas, 33–34
Hall, Stuart, 4
Hanlin Company, 38–39
Haraway, Donna, 5
Harvill, Y. L., 162n11
Hawaii, 22
Heald, Elmer, 73
health care, 60
hegemony, 13. *See also* cultural hegemony
Heller Committee for Research in Social Economics, 120
Henry, William M., 58
Hernández, Dolores, 122
Hernández, Jimeno, 91–92
Hernández, Santana, 37
Hibbard, J. L., 52–53
Hicks Camp (El Monte, Calif.), 116, 118–120
Hill, F. F., 132
"Hindus." *See* farm workers, Asian Indian; immigrants, Asian Indian
Hoffman, Abraham, 78
Hofstadter, Richard, 12
Holcomb, Mrs. S. F., 91–92
Holly Sugar Corporation, 177n44
Holmes Supply Company, 38–39, 52, 58, 159n35
House of Representatives (U.S.), 130, 134, 136. *See also* Congress (U.S.)
housing, 58–66, 68. *See also* camps, labor; living conditions
Huerta, Dolores, 137
Hutchinson, Kan., 37

identity: conflicting concepts of, 4, 148n4; Mexican American crisis of, 97–98; national, 4, 7–8, 45, 47; and selfhood, 4, 148n6; social construction of, 5, 14, 69, 75
illegal immigrants, 44, 80, 82, 99
Illinois, 100
imagined communities, 138, 148n9
immigrants, Armenian, 21. *See also* farm workers, Armenian

immigrants, Asian, 11, 16, 22–23, 25, 30. *See also* farm workers, Asian
immigrants, Asian Indian, 21–22, 25
immigrants, Canadian, 16, 25
immigrants, Chinese, 16, 23, 25, 33, 66, 69. *See also* anti-Chinese agitation; Chinese Exclusion Act of 1882; farm workers, Chinese
immigrants, European, 16, 25, 30. *See also* workers: European American
immigrants, Filipino, 22–23, 25, 68. *See also* anti-Filipino agitation; farm workers, Filipino; repatriation, Filipino
immigrants, illegal. *See* illegal immigrants
immigrants, Indian. *See* immigrants, Asian Indian
immigrants, Japanese, 18, 23, 25, 69. *See also* anti-Japanese agitation; farm workers, Japanese; workers: Japanese
immigrants, Korean, 21–22, 25
immigrants, Mexican: American perceptions of, 6, 51, 75, 77, 135, 155n57; in California, 6, 25–26, 43–44, 111; cultural transition and exchange, 1, 67; deportation and repatriation, 45, 78–79, 100, 114, 116, 139, 169n25; as farm workers, 11, 23–25, 32, 58, 134–135; incentives for migration, 27, 31, 158n22; as industrial workers, 30; prevalence of nuclear family unit among, 139; as railroad workers, 58; as recipients of public relief, 168n23; resistance to domination, 149n10; settlement patterns, 58, 66; studies of, 150n12; in the United States, 1–3, 7, 26, 30, 42–45, 63, 109, 111, 155n2, 156n3. *See also* farm workers, Mexican; Mexican

ABOUT THE AUTHOR

Camille Guerin-Gonzales is an associate professor of history at Oberlin College.